Discovering

SHIBARI

A COMPREHENSIVE GUIDE TO JAPANESE ROPE ARTS AND KINBAKU FOR BEGINNERS

Ken Richards

i

Table of Contents

INTRODUCTION

Shibari is a form of art: an art of ropes. It involves more than just tying knots; it involves feelings, trust, and education. You will discover on this adventure that Shibari is about creating relationships and going through thrilling sequences. The term Shibari represents a Japanese word translated to mean "to tie" or "to bind." However, Shibari (also often referred to as "Kinbaku" or Japanese rope bondage) primarily stands as a Japan-originating contemporary practice involving tying individuals with rope. The origin of Shibari comes from an ancient Japanese martial art for binding captives that has now evolved to be used in different contexts, depending on the motive of individuals.

Central to the Shibari art is tying a person with rope to create knots and patterns that contrast beautifully with the body, accentuating the natural curves of the body (especially the female body). The ropes used in Japanese rope bondage are usually made from naturally occurring fibers such as hemp or jute. The rigger/rope top (individual doing the tying) carefully ties up the bunny/rope bottom (the one being tied up) to produce beautiful ties. Shibari is an art that requires the thoughtfulness and creativity of the rigger, as each tie

ix

should have its peculiar meaning and be beautiful to the eyes. Aesthetics and other individualized motives form the intricacies of the art. A metaphoric comparison of Shibari to painting art would mean the bunny is a canvas, the rope is the paint and brush, and the rigger is the paint artist.

This book aims to enable beginners and a wide variety of Shibari practitioners to grasp the art's superficial and innate elements. Providing accurate information on the history and systematic technique of the art, addressing misunderstandings around the art, and elucidating the art's benefits summarizes this book's focus. As we advance, we are set to explore and understand the world of Shibari.

Chapter One

Understanding Shibari

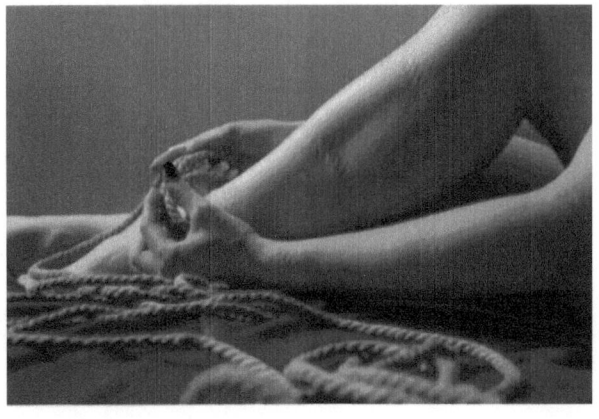

Recently, Shibari art's aesthetics, culture, and mentally stimulating elements have been downplayed and ignored due to a misconception that Shibari is just some sort of kinkiness or sexual play only. Shibari is mostly now considered the "bondage" in BDSM - a sexual practice for bondage, discipline, dominance, sadism, and masochism. It is now sometimes referred to as a game of masochism. This school of thought is largely wrong, as two people who are not romantic partners can easily participate in Shibari as long as the rule of consensualism is not bridged. People can participate in Shibari for diverse reasons, such as mental exercise, relaxation, and sometimes meditation, as done in yoga. It should be known that even though Shibari emerged from secretive scenes of sexual play among ancient Japanese people, the art is not inherently sexual. This is to say that the experience and purpose of Shibari transcends sexual pleasure. It is an art premised on Japanese historical culture characterized by creativity, pleasure, and emotional connection. Because of the unconventional nature of the rope-tying exercise in the art, several other misconceptions of the art have diminished its glory. Such misconceptions range from myths like "Shibari is all about sex" (as mentioned earlier) to other myths that consider Shibari a violent, painful, degrading, and dangerous art. As much as these claims may appear real and somewhat correct in some extreme cases of negligence, it remains valid to say that these talks have arisen from a lack of understanding to a larger extent of lack of participation in the art. Shibari is not a violent or degrading art. It is rather an art that produces pleasure and teaches rigger and bunny humility. It is also not an unsafe art, as rules and precautions are in place to reduce and avert danger. For example, there must be smoothly sharped scissors around where exercise occurs. Safe words and codes are adopted to prompt alertness in extreme situations.

Furthermore, most importantly, there must be a communicated agreement between individuals before beginning the art. Knowledge of all these is paramount to not mis-conceptualize the art. All of these gaps in knowledge are what this work aims to fill.

Misconceptions about Shibari

➢ It is only for sex.

Many people think the reason others practice Shibari is for sexual exploitation. Although Kinbaku is naturally sexy, it rarely ends up grinding and bumping. If it happens, that is okay, but it is not every time people engage in Kinbaku for sex. There are so many reasons to practice Shibari without leading to sex. To some people, Kinbaku is an art. Lots of riggers spend months and years honing their skills. The most popular Shibari practitioners are proficient with their hands and know what their partners like or dislike. To some, the word Shibari explains the art and a fetish practice; you cannot do one without the latter. Activities like performing live or perfecting their style are most important for this set of people. To some, it is a way of creating trust and intimacy with another person. Many rope tops and bottoms are sexual partners in real life, but in some situations, these two only work together on an expert level. Some individuals have play partners who end up being separated from their romantic partners if their loved ones cannot fulfill a particular fetish. Finally, some people participate in Shibari for relaxation and stress relief. Not every time you get tied up. It will be painful.

> ➢ The real name is not Kinbaku.

Shibari is the proper term for Japanese rope bondage. Shibari is the general name in Japanese, which means "tie." Kinbaku is unique and involves weaving intricate knots for suspending and binding people for erotic and art purposes. The name "Shibari" is more accepted internationally because the practice has been adapted or spread to non-Japanese audiences.

> ➢ Those who practice Shibari are not deranged or psychopaths.

It could be accurate, but not for everyone. However, the perception is that everyone who engages in Shibari for sexual pleasure is a sadist, has experienced childhood trauma, or has a mental health issue. Not every person fits a stereotype. Shibari is not all about looks. Shibari fetish models may appear intimidating, but are primarily fun people. They may appear psychopaths, but they are not. For someone interested in the Shibari and who wants to become an expert, rope lovers come from different Social and cultural backgrounds and belong to all types of careers and cliques. A lot of them had childhood experiences filled with love or hatred. It is rare for creepy and freaky people to be present at events related to Shibari, and any person causing discomfort or trouble is thrown out. Abusers who act as rope tops are not allowed. The Shibari community looks out for one another.

➤ It is not very respectful.

Shibari's play is not humiliating. It should not be done in a way that can make someone uncomfortable or disrespected. Shibari should be fun, engaging, and enjoyable. If you do not feel this way after or during, stop or do not engage in it again, and never doubt your feelings. In Shibari, your feelings matter. If you feel uncomfortable, stop. Something that can feel pleasurable or exciting to an individual can be overly uncomfortable. It is unpleasant for someone else, and you do not have to justify the personal experience to another person.

➢ It is dangerous

Shibari may look dangerous, but it is harmless when done correctly. Many safety measures can be implemented since there are many health risks, like suffocation and nerve damage. People who rig ships in a certain way deal with rope masters before suspending or binding another person. They also possess an in-depth knowledge of human anatomy. Well-learned riggers take risks seriously and stay alert while trying to keep the rope bottom secured. Shibari may appear easy for a bottom, but the person is not passive. Rope bottoms are generally fit and flexible, with high pain tolerance. The rigger mainly checks in with the bottom to ascertain they are not in pain. When the bottom's hand begins to feel numb, if they want to stop a scene, they need to express their feelings clearly to the rigger to untie their hands, which can be challenging if floating in subspace. The bottom has a specific control. The onus lies on the top and bottom to work together to make a pleasurable scene. Unfortunately, there are moments when torture gets into the background. Many rope bottoms love to be electrocuted, soaked in hot wax, spanked, or whipped while tied. However, some practices, such as spanking and whipping, are a consensus act and are practiced cautiously.

Why should you tie Shibari?

Shibari is similar to a dance of emotions. Not only are ropes involved, but also vulnerability and mutual trust. Shibari creates a space for partners to reveal their genuine selves and unearth secret areas of their hearts when one person binds and the other is tied.

Other things to know about the Shibari

➢ Shibari demonstrates the value of trust

The one tied trusts the person tying and takes care of the other. Because of their mutual trust, their relationship is deeper and stronger than it otherwise would be. They can better understand one another and explore their shared emotions through Shibari.

➢ Intuition without Words

Shibari does not only communicate with words. The movement of the ropes and how the body reacts develop into communication. It is similar to a partner's private language. They learn to recognize when something feels good or needs to change without expressing themselves aloud.

Brief history of Shibari

Shibari developed from an ancient traditional Japanese martial art called "Hojojutsu." This martial art style was used in Japan within the Senogoku era (mainly 1336-1573) and the Edo period (1600 and mid-1800s) to arrest, bind, and sometimes torture prisoners with ropes or cords. Hojojutsu was a military practice in which the Samurai carefully tied up prisoners in manners that explained their crime status. They were often brought out for public display before incarceration or execution, exposing the art to the general public. In the late 1800s, when the shogunate was displaced and the end of the Edo period came, Hojojutsu tradition also disappeared. However, the people of Japan began to adopt the Hojojutsu tying techniques in their secretive BDSM acts, making Hojojutsu evolve into an art of the decorative, tight, erotic form of rope bondage called "Kinbaku-bi" meaning "the beauty of tight binding." However, this erotic form of rope bondage was restricted to being only an underground occurrence in Japan. Kinbaku did not appear publicly in Japan until artists such as Itoh Seiyu brilliantly combined the techniques of kinkabu with modern art and displayed them publicly. Also, other skilled Kinbaku art performers, such as Akechi Denki and Osada Eikichi, emerged. These performers helped establish Kinbaku as an acceptable art in Japan. In the present day, especially in the western regions, this art of erotic bondage is popularly called Shibari. Kinbaku and Shibari refer to the same type of play and are frequently used interchangeably.

Shibari began to spread outside of Japan in the early 1900s, near World War II, when it started to move into Europe and America. According to Midori (a popular Japanese-American sexologist, educator, and author of "Seductive Art of Japanese Bondage"), some American soldiers witnessed the art during World War II and stealthily took it back to the United States. The art was generously accepted in the Western world by kinky people and began to spread even more. By the late 1990s, Shibari was all over the internet. Today, Shibari has gone across communities and nations and has made its mainstay in the BDSM communities of the 21st century.

9

Cultural Elements of Shibari

The artistic elements of the Shibari art are solely built around Japan and her historical culture. Some apparent conditions of the nation reasonably contributed to the origination of Shibari from Japan. The act of binding is not foreign to the Japanese people. It forms a major part of their daily life. For instance, traditional clothes have no buttons and are usually tied with cloth bands. The use of ropes is also not far-fetched in the Japanese communities. Because of their minimal possession of raw materials such as iron, ropes are used to replace the absence of these materials when possible. Ropes are used for demarcation in their temples, as weapons of torture to obtain military information, and for public punishment of wrongdoers, amongst many others. All these point to the wide availability and application of ropes in Japan and the connection of this to the use of ropes in Japanese bondage art.

In a recent interview in Sydney, Daniel Kok, a present-day skilled Shibari artist, talks about how Shibari art allows for humility in both individuals involved. He says, "It (Shibari) is about giving permission, taking power." "Since becoming an artist, I have tried very hard not to feel the need to have the last word, not to think I am most important, to gain a full understanding of what it means to be responsible for something." This characteristic of Shibari is in simulation with the feeling of humiliation and suffering encountered by the prisoners being tied up in the ancient Hojojutsu art. However, the change in the motive of individuals in Shibari gives a different emotional feeling.

The aesthetic function of ropes in Shibari can also be attributed to the same practice in Japan. The Japanese people have always learned to make beautiful patterns with their ropes. The most valued gifts in Japan are adorned with ritual knots made from ropes. A practice that has been extended to the rope bondage art. The attention given to producing visually appealing patterns of the ties in Shibari is a distinguishing feature of the art.

The cultural background of Shibari has set an aura of uniqueness around the art, making it different from regular Western rope bondage and other forms of bondage art. While it does share some qualities with such arts, differences exist,

11

ranging from the type of material (rope) used to the intent and outcome of the art. Shibari has been commonly compared with Western bondage art. The Western or American bondage art generally refers to the act of bondage in BDSM settings. This form of bondage represents a consensual sexual play involving physical restriction to a person's movement and freedom with ropes, chains, shackles, handcuffs, and other restraining materials. The sole purpose of Western bondage remains erotic pleasure. That forms the intent of the act from the onset. This is quite the contrary in Japanese bondage art. In Shibari, restraining material is limited only to the use of ropes, but the purpose of the art is not limited to sexual pleasure. The acts in Shibari may sometimes be fully represented in BDSM, but the full identity of the art cannot be restricted to BDSM.

Questions also arise from the synonymous use of Shibari. These questions are posed to clarify if there exist differences between both forms of art. From authentic Japanese history, there is no art named Shibari as this is a regular Japanese action word meaning to bind. Still, Kinbaku, on the other hand, represents the art of decorative tight binding that originated after the disappearance of hojojutsu. In the

Western region, the word Shibari predominantly means the art of rope binding. Kinbaku is a more common and definite art representation in Japan than Shibari. This reasonably explains the interchangeable use of both words.

Nevertheless, the art world has not failed to illuminate the hidden nuances between both concepts. Shibari is an art that focuses on Japanese tying techniques and aesthetics. In Shibari, the artist mainly creates beautiful artistic ties on the human body, which may produce a spectrum of several mental and emotional benefits, or sometimes just relaxation and fun. Sexual arousal and gratification can also be created through the process. Kinbaku, however, is constantly an erotic art of bondage. Kinbaku focuses on the emotional and sexual connection between the rope partners.

Unlike other artistic expressions, Shibari is an art beyond the display of beauty and emotions. It connotes a heritage of culture.

Chapter Two

Building a Strong Foundation

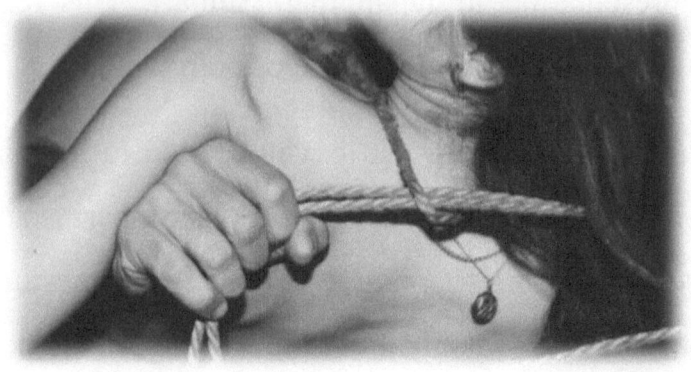

One primary purpose and benefit of rope bondage art is to improve trust and communication between the participants. This invariably suggests that a level of communication and trust exists at the foundation of Shibari. The focus on these fundamentals of human relationships has led to increased participation of people in shiabri, especially romantic partners. It requires a measure of trust to release oneself from being tied by another, trusting the individual's judgment. Beneath this level of trust is a phase of proper communication. Communication involves the personal willingness to perform the act without coercion or threat – consent. The artist (rigger) and client (bunny) or two romantic partners (as the case may be) must individually and collectively consent to participate in the art. Much more than this is an agreement to adhere to specific limits set to the act. This communication must precede the exercise as this forms a mental basis of trust and communication for the entire process. It brings some degree of comfortability to the mind, allowing the individual to ease into the forthcoming experience. The state of Shibari being consensual makes the art not the loose, unethical act it is misconstrued to be. It differentiates it from a military act of torture, suffering, and shame (hojojutsu).

Instructions for both rope bottom and rope top
 ⚔ Instructions for rope bottoms

There are a few things a rope bottom must know before practicing Kinbaku with a rope top. Firstly, you must avoid meeting new people in private places. Secondly, instead of just getting to know only about your rope top, get to know a few of his friends in the environment and learn about his skills and reputation. Finally, before you meet a stranger to perform Kinbaku, inform a close friend and check in with that friend once you return. Tell them to look into it once you fail to check in with your friend.

15

✓ Choose a partner carefully:

Before going into Kinbaku and just allowing any rope top to tie you up, use the following to evaluate them;

✓ Who has the other party tied before? What is their reputation in the community?

Please learn about your rope top from the community instead of meeting them in private rooms. This would allow you to talk to people who might know the rope top and tell you some information about them.

✓ How experienced is the rope top

Most people may state that experience does not equal that individual's skill level. This factor is still important to know because if your rope top is a novice in Kinbaku, you can use this as an opportunity to learn with your rope top.

✓ Is the other party knowledgeable about bondage safety?

You must ensure that your rope top knows more than you on Kinbaku. To know this, you must also know about Kinbaku, then take it with your rope top. After conversing with them, you would know if they do not know much about Kinbaku, and you would consider entrusting your safety with them. You can also confirm if they possess safety items like trauma shears.

✓ Finally, you need to know yourself:

Yes, knowing all about the safety instructions and rules in Kinbaku, but it is also essential to know about your body. Press on the part of your body and find out where your nerve bundles are. Figure out the places on your body that can feel tingly quickly and places that can endure the highest amount of force. We have different people. Some people's thighs are part of the body that is the strongest. At the same time, some people would start feeling tingly and aching once they lift their limbs. So, every rope top must be able to adjust to its rope bottom perfectly. Every rope bottom's flexibility is different.

✓ Do you have any body injury?

Another important factor you need to know about your body before entering Kinbaku is if you have any injuries. The injuries might be old or new; you must consider them. Tell your rope top about some areas they must avoid during Kinbaku or if you have any psychological issues. Before going into this art, here are some questions you need to ask yourself: Did you have any unpleasant experiences in Kinbaku? Do you have any physical challenges? Do you have some personal stuff that makes you nervous? Do you not like to be touched in some areas? You need to know so many questions about yourself that your rope top would find very useful. The thing about skilled nawashi is that they are skilled enough to adjust to the comfort of their rope bottom, even if the rope bottom has scoliosis. They can find a safe posture for every rope bottom if they know it earlier.

Remember to do warm-ups before any Kinbaku session to reduce your chances of sustaining an injury. Also, eat before any session because being tied up on an empty stomach is not advisable. Many models may be worried that their stomachs might protrude after eating, which might not be suitable for the session. Well, it is much more important to eat before any Kinbaku session because it ensures a great session.

⚓ Instructions for rope tops

The rope top must follow the basic etiquette of the BDSM communities. Some do not join another's play without being adequately invited, and some do not touch others without consent.

Do not just assume that someone would love to do so with you because you saw someone play in a way with another person. If your play in Kinbaku is domination and submission, setting a safe word your partner would say when they feel uncomfortable is appropriate, so you stop the play.

✓ Building the mental aspects of bondage:

When you are meeting with your rope bottom for the first time, do not just go straight into the play; first, to know more about them. Know their physical conditions, and ask them questions like: Have they been tied before? Have they been injured? How high are their flexibility and endurance? What is their emotional response under pressure? Their answers depend on their experiences because some may be unaware of their limitations during Kinbaku.

Before you start Kinbaku, you must give your rope bottom an idea of what you will do or the bondage you are about to practice. Mentally prepare them for what you are about to do so that it will be easier for them to cooperate with you later. Sometimes, you want to surprise your rope bottom, but the

19

rope must have informed the rope bottom earlier of the risks involved, the discomfort they might feel, and the marks they might see on their bodies.

During Kinbaku, instead of turning the rope bottom in so many directions, you should move your body to avoid the bottom from feeling dizzy. When pulling on the rope next to your rope bottom's body, you must use your hand to cover the skin to prevent injuries and bruises. All these rules I have stated show respect to the rope bottom, which you would need their full consent, and are not planning to cause discomfort. Letting them know that you plan to make them feel the most pleasure is essential.

Finally, as the rope top, you must constantly pay attention to the physical condition of your rope bottom. Ensure you are not ignoring the warning signs they might be giving due to aches, tingling sensations, and numbness. During bondage, you must protect the rope bottom from outside interruptions not discussed earlier. For example, you involve other people in touching your rope bottom. Ensure you are within reach of first aid in emergencies.

    ✓ Location and equipment:

Once the temperature is low, the rope bottom's endurance and flexibility would also reduce. Likely, you may not notice the drop in temperature in the room because your temperature may increase due to your activities.

During an emergency, it is possible that the rope bottom might not be able to save themselves after they have been tightly bound. So you must know that the rope bottom's safety is in your hands. So, when practicing Kinbaku at a location unfamiliar to you, ensure you find an escape route or similar information. It is also better if you have equipment that you could use to cut the rope during an emergency within your reach. The best equipment is trauma shears. They might not look sharp but can cut through ropes and clothing.

When the rope top pulls on the overhead knot during a partial suspension, most people wonder if the rope may break. This is not impossible, especially if the hemp rope is old. Once the rope has already attained wear and tear, the top should remove that rope and change it to a new one. During a suspension, though, it is always supported with more than one rope, reducing the chances of one rope breaking.

The most common risk during suspension is the suspension point. This point must be tied around a strong, secure beam or drilled into a wall and booted on the opposite side. There is one problem that a rope top might have: they do not know much about the anchor point, like if the person who installed the anchor point checked out the load bearing or if the anchor point itself has worn out. So, to overcome this problem, you need to learn more about the anchor point installed before using it.

Some things might look sturdy but are actually for decorations and cannot bear weight. For example, because doors and coat hangers are studied does not make them fit to suspend a person. Ensure you use only instruments designed to suspend, such as the **carabiners**. Many items can look like carabiners but are only for decorations and cannot be used in suspension.

Preparing for a Shibari Session

The intricacies of the Shibari art make proper preparation expedient before its performance. It should be performed correctly to harness the emotional power in this art. The preparedness of both parties in this cannot be over-emphasized. Following the decision to participate in Shibari at the beginner's level, a proper orientation on the basic concepts of Shibari is done. This must include all that needs to be known about the art. The rules, guidelines, precautions, and risks associated with experience are also mentioned. In the next phase, there will be discussions about their personal preferences, unique expectations, and boundaries. This is to set a ground for openness and respect. At this stage, the intent of each part should be communicated as the motive drives the force of the art and determines the results. The expectations from the session will also set the ambiance throughout the rope-tying process. From the point of orientation to discussion, trust is already being cultivated in the minds of each party. However, this can be more intentional by carrying out trust-building exercises and guiding the bunny through possible advanced Shibari techniques that can be encountered. In summary, the state of mind of both individuals must be ready for the adventure they are about to go on. An environment of vulnerability, openness, and trust must be achieved before the art begins.

The preparation of the physical space for Shibari should also not be neglected. This would involve a series of preventive activities of the individuals and the physical area to be used. Artists will teach clients stretches and exercises that will increase flexibility and reduce the chances of physical injuries, such as losing blood flow to some parts of the body. These exercises also keep the body fit, building up the body's strength and endurance limits. Other physical preparations will include essential safety measures that will reduce the risks of danger during shabari sessions. One simple safety measure will be to always have safety scissors beside to set the bunny free as soon as possible if there may be any emergencies. Safe words and codes are also welcomed.

Essential Safety Guidelines in Shibari

Shibari is an art endangered with physical risks. It will require prompt adherence to rules to avert or minimize these risks. In Shibari, both individuals have a responsibility to each other; hence, it is important to follow the guidelines to ensure the safety of the other is not threatened. They have roles to play together and individually. Individuals should focus on ensuring the other party is also doing the needful. It is not out of place to still emphasize the importance of communication. The rigger should also communicate his abilities, experiences, boundaries, and vice versa. Ensure there is a feeling of comfort and trust between the partners, especially when any of the individuals is a newbie. The art area should be widely spaced and dry (spills on the floor). No two people under the influence of alcohol must participate in Shibari. Rigger and Bunny must be sober.

The bunny must check within herself and ascertain a good mental. No claustrophobia or panic with ropes. There must be mention to the rigger of any previous injuries that may cause pain or affect the ties. Immediately, if there is a feeling of numbness, coldness, or burning around limbs, it should be reported to the rigger. Bunny can speak up if needed to be out of rope. Whatever the reason, it should not be offensive to the rigger.

Riggers should use ropes from jute and hemp as these are the choice materials for Shibari. Compared to other synthetic ropes, these ropes are strong but soft on the skin (especially when treated). Ropes must be treated by boiling, dried, and then oiled before use. Before tying someone, the rigger should observe for baseline color and temperature. If a change in color or coldness is noticed after tying, the particular tie should be loosened. Rigger should find a means of communication with the bottom to ensure they are doing okay. Ropes should not be tied under the armpits or knots behind the knee, inner wrist, or thighs. If there is any numbness, the bottom should rotate, open, and close their arms or wriggle their toes to restore blood circulation. If numbness remains, ropes should be cut calmly with scissors.

Safety issues

❖ Things to consider during the selection of which body part to tie:

While practicing Kinbaku, knowing which part of the body to tie is very important. We all know that the safest place to tie a rope is on the parts with thick muscles or sturdy places. The most dangerous place to tie a rope is on nerves or blood vessels because they are shallow. A list of places that are safe to tie on the body and some precautions include;

❖ The Wrist

You can tie it around the wrist, where you would find the radial and ulnar bones joined to the wrist. The wrist is fragile due to the groove on the inside. There are shallow blood vessels in the wrist, so you have to adjust the rope in this position when tying.

❖ The Waist and Hip

The waist and hip are other safe body parts to tie. Tie your rope to the narrower hip area so the rope will not come loose. Tying your rope here is much safer, especially when the feet are above the head. Some rope bottoms find it more comfortable to tie the rope on their hip bone, especially during suspensions with larger forces. As you may know, the hip bone is solid, and once you tie your rope, it can lower the rope bottom's center of gravity and protect internal organs.

❖ The Leg

The following body part that is safe to tie is the leg. When tying around the ankle, the tie should be wide and adjusted so there would be no lateral tip.

❖ The Arm

The following body part you can tie is the arm. Our arm's elbow is fragile and has shallow nerves and blood vessels. Due to this, it is much better to tie a rope to the forearm. When tying the forearm, avoid the armpits. This is because this is the passage for the nerves that connect the arm to the torso. Tying a rope directly on the armpits would constrict the nerves, making the rope bottom feel numb.

❖ The neck

You might be skeptical that tying a rope around that region might be dangerous for this body part. Well, it is not once you properly tie your rope. The neck has carotid arteries passing through both sides and a windpipe in the middle. Working with this region of the body is very dangerous. A rope at both sides of the neck can compress the carotid arteries, and a knot in the middle might impede breathing.

How to make your partner feel pleasure in your first attempt.

You must learn to apply force while tying and become comfortable with the rope. Some may get caught up in how the rope moves and become lost. You tend to neglect your partner once you pay too much attention to the technique. Different techniques are used in Kinbaku to make your partner feel pleasure, but the most important thing is to memorize how the rope moves.

This session explains how to make your partner feel pleasure while using Kinbaku since we know Kinbaku is all about expressing sexual desire and love to your partner. Firstly, you must ensure that you and your partner are mutually enjoying the experience because playing with rope can be done with no technique but cannot be done without the spirit. The technique involves using one rope without making any knots. It is the one-rope technique.

- Firstly, use a quiet, relaxing, and comfortable location. The place has to be quiet because it is ideal to hear each other's breathing and the sound of the rope.
- After selecting the place, unbundle a rope and place it there.
- Take your rope, press up against the bottom, and press your chest into her back. Make sure you are feeling each other's breathing.
- Next, extend your arm over her shoulder and use your body's temperature to relax her body.
- Move her softly and guide her to stretch out her limbs and body.
- Then, you use the rope to your advantage and bring the bundle to her ear.

- Squeeze the bundle and let her hear the rope bottom hitting each other.
- Next, pull the rope head to undo the bundo and let the rope drop on the floor to make a melodious sound.

  You then hold your rope and press it against the rope bottom's skin and then trace it across her neck and shoulders. Then, pull on the rope, rub it against her skin, and move it back and forth several times.
- Use your thumb and your index finger to open the rope head.
- Then, use those two fingers to hook your rope from the outside to the inside.
- Then, pull on the rope to form a loop. It is called the cow hitch.
- Once this hitch is done, you pass the hand of your rope bottom through the loop, hold the rope tail end, and pull.
- Wrapping the loop around the rope bottom's forearm is much better than her wrist.

- Then, wrap the rope around the rope bottom's body and change the speed and force used when wrapping her body the second and third times.

- You then wrap other parts of your rope bottom's body and practice expressing your emotions as you wrap. For example, a wrap can express closeness and love, while another can express longing and desire.

- Your wraps can express many emotions, so you use them to let your rope bottom know your emotions.

- Since you are using a single rope, it can be used up easily. So you untie your partner and wrap her again at a different part of her body.

- One thing about Kinbaku is that untying is more important than tying. This is because as you untie, you have to keep pressing against her so she can feel your body temperature as you untie her.

- While untying, you can cover her sensitive areas or press on them.

- Make sure you give your rope bottom erotic caresses. Then, use your rope to stimulate sensitive parts and squeeze her breasts so they can stand out.

- Use minimal techniques, like only hooking a rope around her body parts. Just flow with her body, not the rope. Doing this would enable you to focus on your partner's body and all her responses.
- Caressing her body using your rope or your hands would give different sensations.
- You can use the rope to press on covered or uncovered private areas on her body based on what you agreed to before.

Chapter Three

Rope Selection and Maintenance

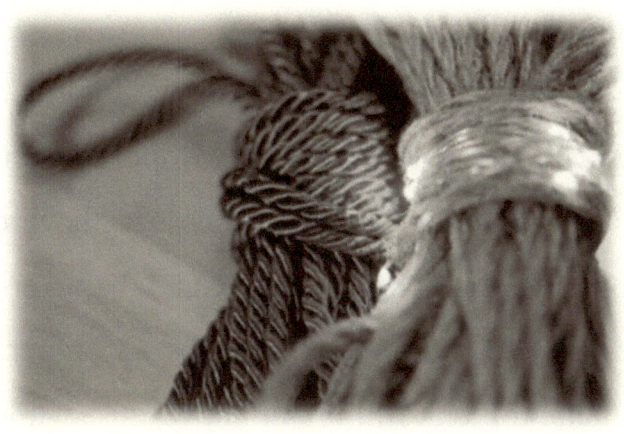

The foundation for secure and efficient rope use is laid forth in the Introduction to Rope Selection and Maintenance. Care rope selection is essential to ensure the task's optimum material, strength, and properties. Performance, safety, and longevity are all affected. Maintaining a rope is equally important for avoiding wear and damage and assuring its dependability. These procedures are widely accepted throughout industries, including the maritime and industrial sectors, to avoid chaffing deterioration and guarantee trustworthiness in hoisting and rigging operations. The rope function is guaranteed to be at its best, and its lifespan is increased by being aware of the extent of rope maintenance.

Smearing this understanding to Shibari ensures a safe and enjoyable encounter.

Guidelines for Rope Selection

Guidelines for choosing ropes have improved due to developments in rope materials. Rope selection is still influenced by material, diameter, and strength, with materials like polypropylene having special characteristics like toughness and resistance to the elements. Comparing natural and synthetic ropes is still important because while synthetic ropes (nylon, polyester) offer more strength and less stretching, natural ropes (jute, hemp) are better suited for traditional aesthetics. Recent developments have allowed users to customize their experience by understanding how rope flexibility and texture affect comfort and handling. Exploring diverse rope materials has increased because of cutting-edge synthetics like polypropylene, which offer adaptable solutions for various applications. Advancements addressing certain requirements, such as high-strength ropes for heavy lifting, which profit from polyester and polypropylene, influence modern rope choices. These developments ensure that choosing a rope aligns with certain requirements, improving performance and safety.

Factors to Consider in Rope Selection

Considerations for choosing a rope include various crucial elements for its safe and efficient use. Ropes are made to endure particular forces and loads. Therefore, safety concerns and load-bearing capacity are crucial. For endurance and continuous performance, rope durability and lifespan are essential, especially in applications like hoisting and rigging. User experience is influenced by sensory factors, including comfort and feeling, which make ropes comfortable to wear and use. With color and visual appeal enhancing the whole experience and enabling personalization, aesthetics is increasingly valued.

Notably, these aspects apply to various industries, including building and material handling, where wire ropes must meet rigid safety requirements and support a range of loads. Research also looks at how different wear scar forms affect fracture failure behavior and bearing capacity, emphasizing the importance of durability. Together, these factors affect the selection of rope to ensure safe, enduring performance in various applications.

Types of Ropes Suitable for Shibari

Choosing the right ropes in Shibari is essential to creating secure and aesthetically beautiful bonds.

Choosing rope for Shibari and other types of rope bondage

You have a wide variety of ropes that you can use. Most of it all comes down to preference, what you prefer to tie with, and what the model likes. But, again, that goes back to the consent; you can not force a particular type of rope on them if they do not have a preference.

There are three categories;

1. synthetics like nylon,
2. organics like jute, hemp, bamboo, and
3. cotton.

For suspension, hemp, jute, and bamboo are primarily used because they are firm. The advent of synthetic fibers allowed standing and aesthetic Shibari to bounce out and become a little more eye-capturing.

Cotton is easy to use and find because it is a ubiquitous fiber. However, it is soft but not firm and, when pulled too taut, can be a little restrictive. The primary width of the rope is between 6 and 8 millimeters (mil); when pulled tight, cotton tends to get slightly lower than the 6 millimeters. It can become too constrictive if it becomes too thin; constriction is the enemy of comfort. Unless the model wants the discomfort, then use more caution.

Many people ask, what sort of rope is recommendable for them?

It is not a simple answer and, possibly even more confusing with many rope choices. It will be like anything else, a very individual thing. One isn't necessarily better than the other, although there is nasty rope and nice rope. And like all things in life, we get what we pay for. The other thing is that the individual will begin to appreciate the difference as the skills increase. Like anything, be it musical instruments, tools, or whatever, a better quality product gives a better result. And it is just nicer to use and easier to handle.

For many people, a rope is a rope. They only perceive the difference as the color, the diameter, and possibly the material, which is not always easy to tell. We can divide the rope into types according to the construction.

Braided Rope

Many beginners will get a braided rope like this.

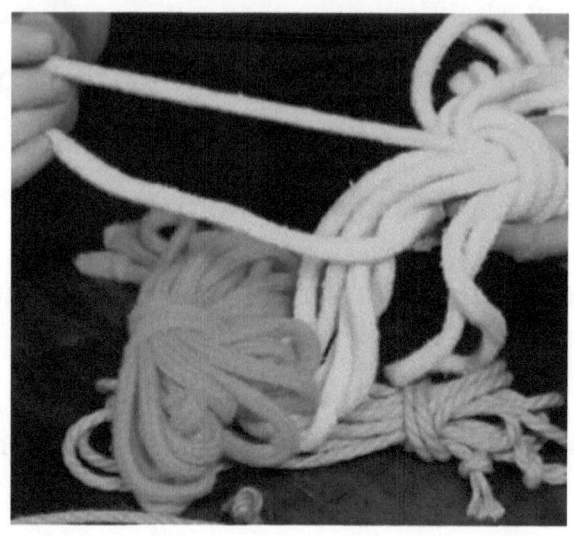

These tend to be either made out of cotton or synthetic. There is nothing wrong with these for an essential sort of bedroom bondage. It is pretty strong, but cotton is not strong enough, and it is not an ideal rope except for bedroom bondage floor work.

One thing that is quite nice about it is that it is very soft. But unfortunately, it has a little stretch, which is not great because knots can get very tight. So it is one of those times the person might need the safety shears. Always have some safety scissors with you just in case you need to snip some of the ropes. You can always get a new rope, but you cannot get a new life. So be sure to practice these things in a proper state of mind and consensual.

So the ropes are cheap and cheerful, probably some of the most inexpensive ropes you can get. But it is not a severe Shibari rope unless used for a particular purpose. The stretch makes it strange to work with for things like suspension. So that is the braided, and it's not a twist by the braided finish.

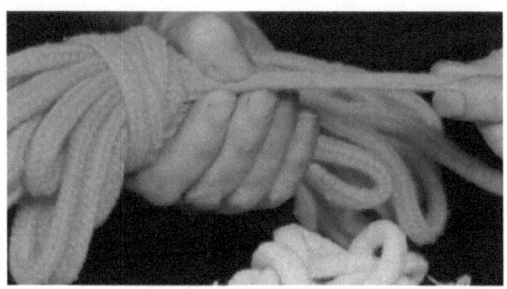

It is a bit like mountaineering rope, and again, that is very stretchy, so it's not an excellent bondage rope.

Twisted rope

The next most common thing is the twisted rope, which most professionals use for Shibari and fusion styles, and so on.

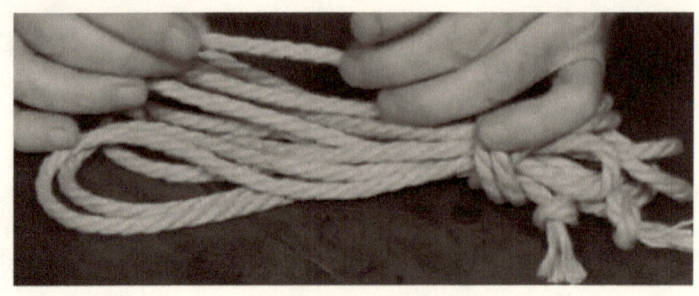

It is a more intense bondage rope mainly because it does not tend to stretch. And it leaves rather nice indents on the skin, particularly the more clearly defined ones. In addition, it shows the lovely patterns after the rope comes off, which disappear very quickly, not to be confused with rope burns, which are another subject.

A rope burn, if pulled fast across somebody's skin, the friction causes it to heat up. That is much more common with synthetics. The users do not tend to get it with natural fiber unless they pull the rope fast. So, getting rope burns with the natural fiber is probably a sign of bad handling and usage. You might get some slight friction marks or grazing on the top layer of skin. But that is not a rope burn; that is something different, like a friction mark or something like that.

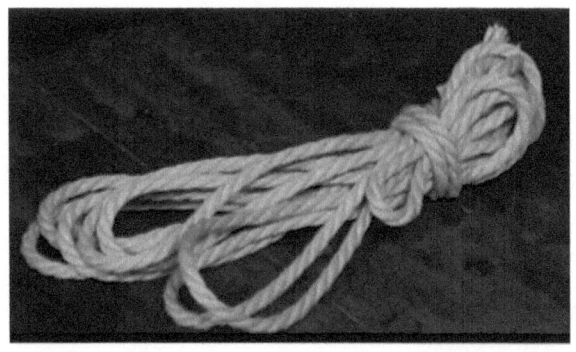

So twisted ropes typically are what we call three plies. In other words, they are made of three bundles of yarn twisted together.

Sometimes, you get four bundles of yarn, a four-ply, which is not ordinary, and nothing wrong with it. So, a bit of a rarity four-ply, and most of the stuff you will come across is three-ply.

So, what makes the difference between different rope materials? Ropes will be divided really into two main types,

Hemp rope

Hemp includes linen hemp, which is flax. Not what people typically refer to or think of as hemp, the cannabis hemp is an industrial version of the stuff people smoke. It does not have the active ingredient in it, or not to any level anybody would ascertain.

That is the one type because of the association with cannabis, and people tend to smoke. There is much legislation regarding the growing of it irrespective of the amount of THC contained.

Flax rope

Some countries have had problems legally growing hemp. In many cases, the alternative will be flax, the same fiber in the linen of bed sheets.

It is just a question of how far the yarn has been refined. What is nice about that is that it tends to cause fewer allergy problems. For example, some people have jute and hemp allergies. However, it is not heard that many people have an allergy to linen sheets. So, the rope is a good choice if you are a little bit sensitive to plant fibers, particularly hemp and jute.

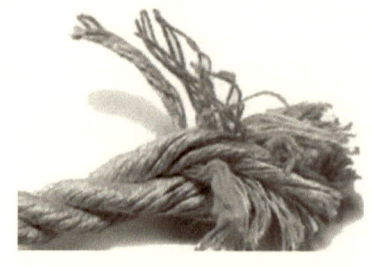

So, it is a very different breed from traditional hemp, which can often be quite a crude product. This is not to say there are no high-grade cannabis hemp ropes, but many tend to have a meager yarn count. For example, three yarns are bundles of yarns but are not highly twisted if pulled apart.

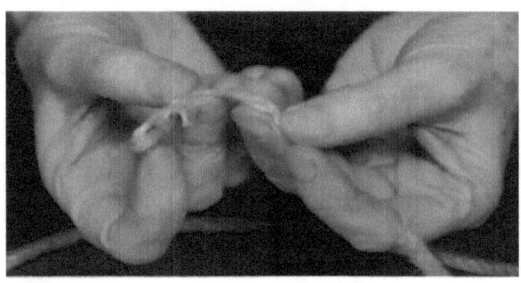

It is one yarn, not multiple thin yarns twisted together, meaning the rope's surface is poorly defined.

And particularly where you have thick yarns, if they are not precisely made, you will get lumps and bumps, and the whole rope will not have such a nice smooth feel when you pull it through your fingers.

Natural fibers

So, we have jute rope on the side of the natural fibers. Jute rope has a twisted structure.

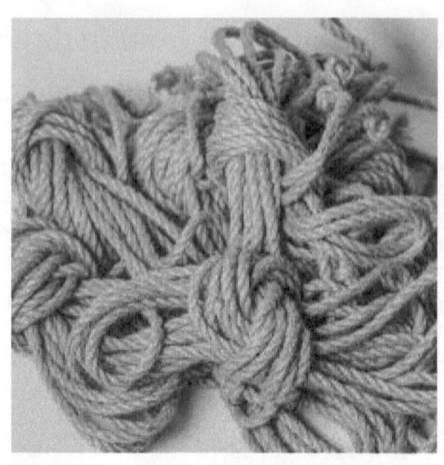

The twisted structure creates excellent knot stability. It is very water-sensitive, so it should not get washed too often. You should not wash it even once to ensure you will not lose carrying capacity. Clean it instead with a piece of cloth and some disinfectants after use.

The second rope on the side of the natural fibers is hemp rope. Hemp rope also has a twisted structure and excellent knot stability. It appears a little more grayish in color, while jute rope appears more golden.

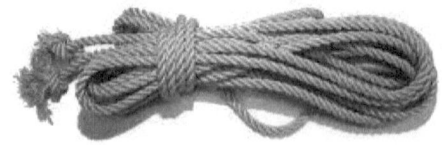

The third rope on the site of the natural fibers is cotton rope. In contrast to jute and hemp ropes, the cotton rope has a plaited structure. The braided design will expand on tension. Therefore, the cotton rope is unsuitable for suspension because it will expand. Then, the knots will get compressed, and it will be hard to untie their knots.

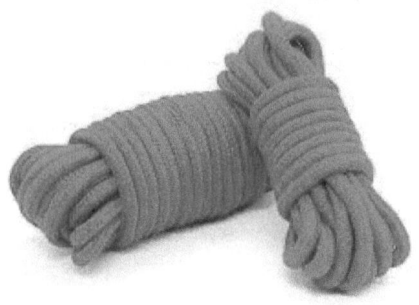

A considerable advantage of cotton rope is that it is often washable without a significant loss of carrying capacity and is very soft to the touch. So, it is suitable for sex or decorative bondage but unsuitable for suspension.

The types of natural ropes include;

- Hemp
- Jute
- Bamboo

- Cotton

- Coconut.

Jute is very commonly used. It is pretty and looks great in photos. It has a distinct smell. It is a great choice. The breaking strength of jute will be about 200 to 300 pounds for a 6-millimeter rope that is brand new. Jute is a very stiff fiber.

Hemp is solid in comparison to jute. Hemp has around 400 to 500 pounds of breaking strength. It is dyed in different forms and colors. It is not as rough as jute. Hemp is nice, loose, and soft. It has a unique sort of odor, too.

Cotton. It is not as big as 6 millimeters. It is slightly smaller. It is very affordable and comes in lots of colors too.

Disadvantages of natural ropes

Natural ropes are not easy to clean. Sometimes, it could run through a flame to take away the little fibers. If you get your rope played gross and dirty, you might have to throw it away. If you wash your rope or you have to wash your rope, different ways are precise ways to do so. These natural fibers absorb water, and you can mess up your rope. Another thing is that they will require a lot more inspection and much scholarly work.

The most common thickness of the rope is 6 millimeters quarter inch. Some may use 4 millimeters for decorative applications. Some may use millimeters because it would allow for more area on the body. What you want to use it for depends on what thickness you will use. The most common length is 30 feet. Some people will need less than 30 feet, or some may need more. Some may need a henk, which is like a bundle of rope. If you are into corsets and you want to tie corsets, and you do not want to have all the knots, you can use the 50 feet. Many people cut the rope to different sizes. You can purchase a pre-made rope, or you can purchase and condition it and up again.

Synthetic ropes

At the site of the synthetic fibers, we have polypropylene ropes. They may appear like a hemp rope, but actually, they are plastic, and you can see that at the ends of the rope where they are melted. So, this plastic rope is unsuitable for rope bondage because it is very stiff and can easily create rope burn on your partner's skin when you pull it too fast over the skin. So, it would help if you did not use it for rope bondage or suspension. But it can be a good option for water bondage because it is not damageable by water, and you can wash it as often as you want.

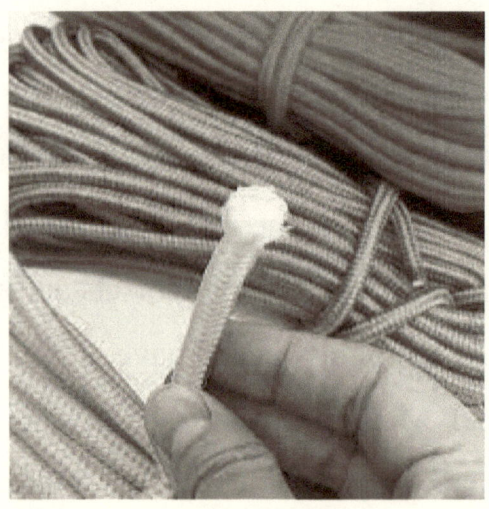

Nylon rope has a plaited structure and the same disadvantages as cotton rope.

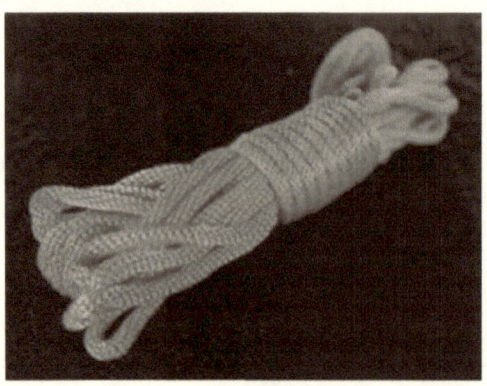

It expands on tension and is unsuitable for suspensions because the knots will get compressed and be hard to untie. Also, it easily creates rope burn because it is a synthetic fiber. However, it is washable as often as you want without substantial loss of carrying capacity. It is very soft to touch.

If you strive for Shibari or suspension, you should choose between jute or hemp. There are significant differences in usability between jute and hemp, but you should choose for your personal preferences. They differ in color, weight, and smell; it is personal preference. If you want to do floor or sex bondage, you can also choose cotton rope or nylon rope, but please be careful if you use nylon rope because of rope burn.

It is an excellent compromise to have enough rope to start a tie already but not too much to be focused only on pulling the rope. Most people will individualize the length of the rope to the partners over time.

The standard diameter of the rope is about five or six millimeters, which is thick enough to carry a body and thin enough to make stable and flat knots. If you have a more extensive body, we do not recommend using thicker rope because your knots will come out bulky and make pressure marks. If you have a more considerable body, you can use more wraps but do not use thicker ropes. If your rope starts to fray or is unequally twisted, you should sort it out. And do not use it anymore, especially not for suspension, because it is unsafe and its carrying capacity has decreased.

An old rope may have many frays and is quite unequally twisted. It would be a rope you can use for sex or floor bondage but not for suspension.

Advantages of synthetic rope.

- They are easy to clean.
- They are smooth and soft.
- They come in lots of colors, even UV colors.
- They are very long-lasting.
- They are very affordable in comparison to some of the natural ropes.
- It is suitable for water bondage because it does not tend to shrink or expand with water. It holds up pretty well when you are using it for water applications.
- It has less reaction to the skin. If you are allergic to some of these natural grasses, using a synthetic rope is a must.

– The breaking strength of synthetic ropes is generally 1000 to 1200 pounds when it is brand new.

Disadvantages of synthetic rope

– One of the disadvantages of synthetic rope is that it can burn you worse than natural rope, like jute, if you pull too much. Be cautious.

The difference is that synthetic rope can be reliably rated because of the manufacturing process. A natural rope is subject to many more variables in manufacturing and wear and tear over time.

Types of synthetic rope

1. Nylon: It is pretty and shiny. It comes in lots of colors. It feels nice on the skin. Some people may do a hybrid and put the natural rope on the body, and then the upline will be a synthetic rope. Natural ropes cannot be reliably rated.

2. Hempex: It is also called a polypropylene three-strand rope. You can use hemp for your uplines. Uplines go from harnesses to the attachment point. It is cheap and

robust. It looks a little bit like jute. It is a popular option.

3. Posh is beautiful. It is a spun polyester. It comes in lots of colors.

More on choosing ropes

The other thing to consider when buying rope is the diameter. Again, stick to something between six and seven millimeter for the best feel and the neatest size knots. But, again, it will be very much down to personal preference and the size of the bodies you are tying.

For instance, tying somebody very tiny in a big, thick seven-millimeter rope or something or even an eight-millimeter rope will look ridiculous and out of proportion. Likewise, tying a very large-bodied person with a five-millimeter rope might look like they are again tied up with dental floss. The question of proportion depends on what feels right in your hands. But five and a half feels just about right, just about perfect. Six feels a little bit bulky.

The difference in knots between using a thicker or a thinner rope can also be a matter of comfort.

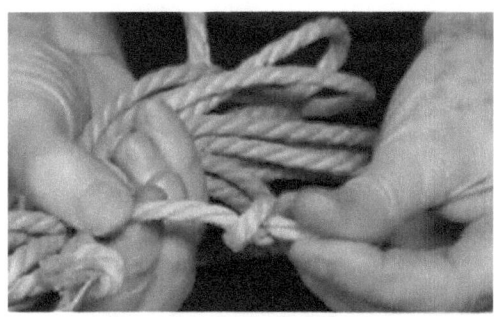

If you are lying on a golf ball-sized knot, it will be much less comfortable than something smaller. However, even that will compress down if a new rope has never been used, treated, or had any load.

For example, we are probably looking at a rope here of about five and a half millimeters and one closer to eight millimeters.

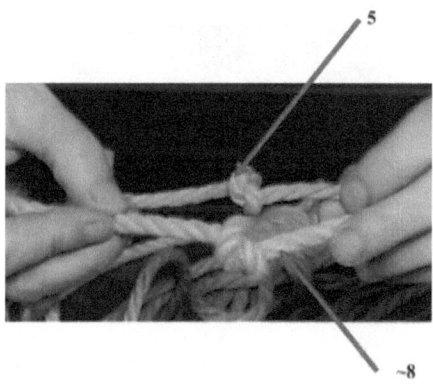

There is a big difference in the size of the knots, which will change how the whole tie looks. The other thing about the giant rope is that it is pretty stiff, dense, and quite tightly twisted. So, even if pulled hard, you can still see daylight through the knot.

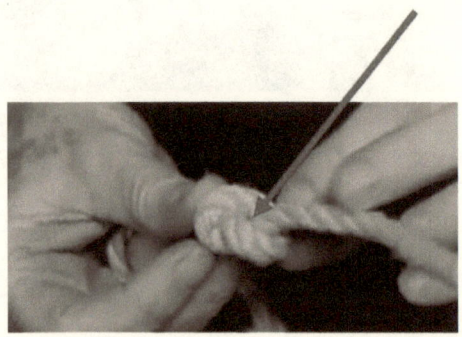

With the thinner rope, because it is much softer, the knot is tightly closed, and there is no daylight in the knot there, and you cannot see through it at all. So it is wholly compacted, and when a knot packs like that, it tends to stay put better.

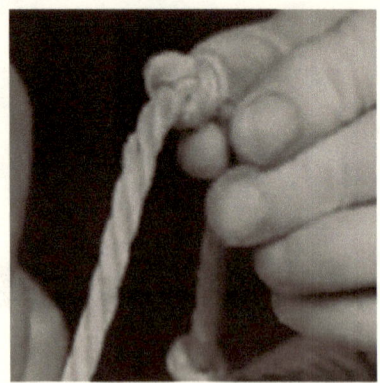

There is friction because all faces meet, which is a good thing. However, friction is essential, particularly for traditional-style Shibari rather than Western-style stuff, because it relies a lot on friction. So, like all things, the rope will depend very much on the quality of the yarn used, that is, yarn quality.

The rope (image below) is consistent; minimal hair is on it, and no dark brown barky bits are sticking out. It is a very clean fiber.

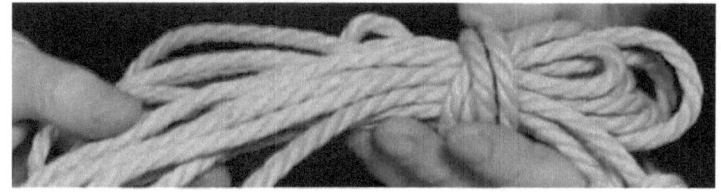

And there are no faults in the manufacturing because the yarns in this are delicate. You will not get any lumps or bumps; they are tiny little fibers. So, if you get any variants in fiber, it will get lost amongst the others.

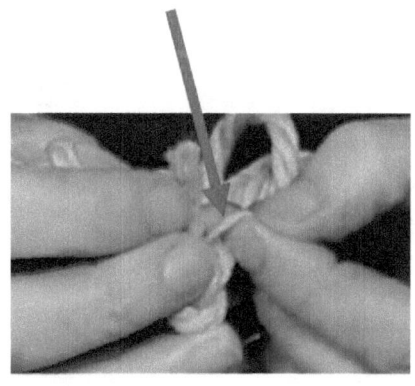

But if you have a small number of yarns and you get a lump, bump, or a bit of foreign fiber, like dark barky bits, it will create an irregularity. So that is the best fiber; you will never find any dark bits in it, and it will always be perfect.

This is some rough, gnarly rope on the other end of the scale.

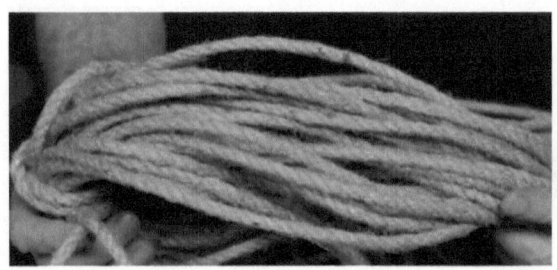

It is a cheap rope, and the manufacturing quality is not excellent. In addition, a significant dark barky bit is sticking out, which you will probably want to remove if you use a rope like this.

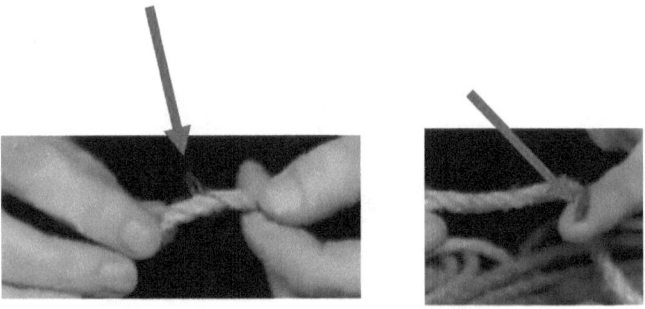

It is not unusual in sort of medium-grade ropes or, in fact, anything but the very best. It is common to find the odd little dark fiber, but this is very inconsistent.

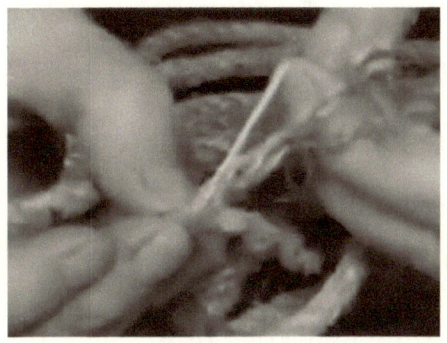

The thickness varies, and some of the bundles of yarn are completely different diameters, creating bulges and irregularities in the rope.

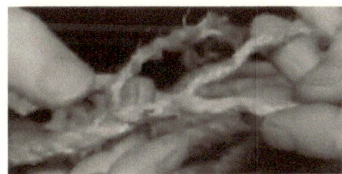 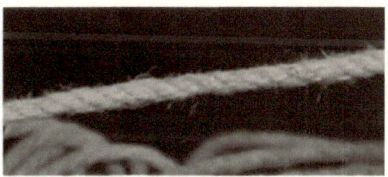

So cheap is not always good; it can be a false economy. It is worth getting something of reasonable quality; the lowest grade is the budget rope.

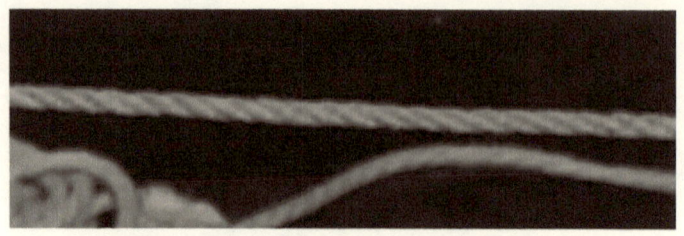

That is a lot cleaner even though you will get some little dark bits in it, but not so many. There is nothing you cannot carefully remove, and you may also notice that the rope is a lot hairier. However, it does come up surprisingly nicely when you have picked your little black bit out and given it oil and a burn.

The picture below is the same rope that has been oiled and burned.

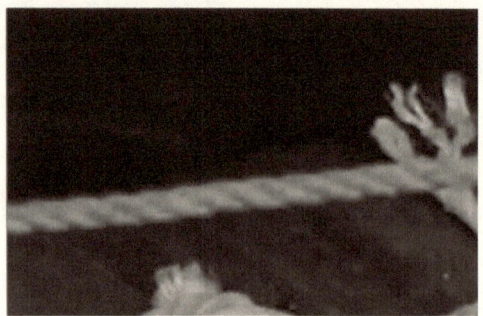

Boiling and burning are also known as dry treating. In other words, take a cloth with oil or wax, pull it down the rope, and just put a small deposit on it.

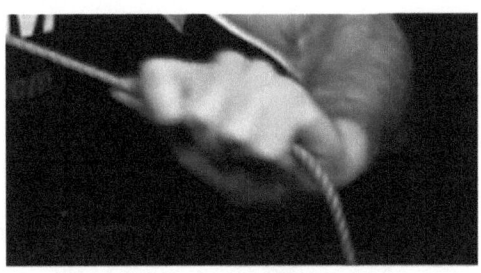

Do not saturate it; then take it and run it over a gas flame. Preferably, use a cooker or a camping stove. Do not use candles because they create soot that will come off onto you and your partner with the rope. So gas is the best way forward- but if you want an inexpensive rope, this is undoubtedly one worth bearing in mind, and it does start to polish and get rather nice with use. It is also very light and very flexible.

The other thing that has quite a significant effect on how the rope feels is the lay. That is just a technical term for the twist rate: how tightly the rope is twisted. For example, in this rope, the twist is very gentle.

It is a very loose lay; in other words, the angle of these twists is relatively flat. On the other hand, a tight lay looks more like this (image below), where there are more twists to the inch, the centimeter, or whatever you use to measure things.

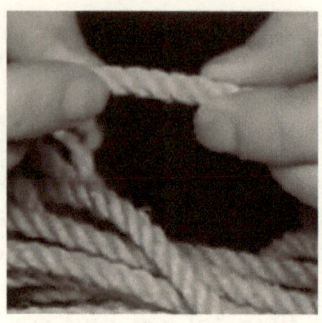

In other words, the twists are more vertical than running parallel to the rope, which is a much sharper angle.

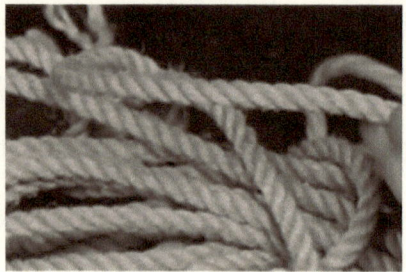

The difference it makes is the degree of flexibility. A stiff piece of linen hemp supports itself under its weight. Initially, it's stiff until broken in, like the stiffness you get on new jeans, a new shirt, or something else. It means the rope is quite hard and does not compress easily.

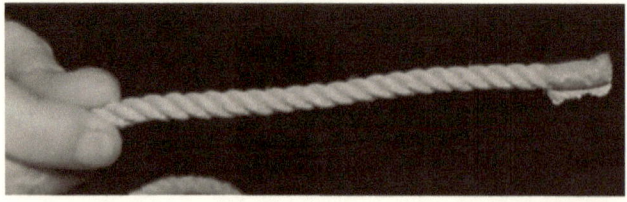

Why would anybody want a tightly laid or hard-laid rope?

If it is stiffer and feels harder, it lasts much longer and is much more forgiving for beginners. But if you compare that now with lighter ropes, such as the tosser light, that is quite flexible.

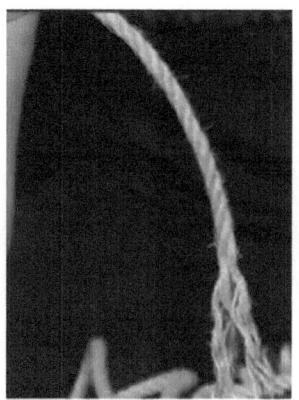

And if you compare it with the super flexible rope, it also compresses more, even at a short length like that.

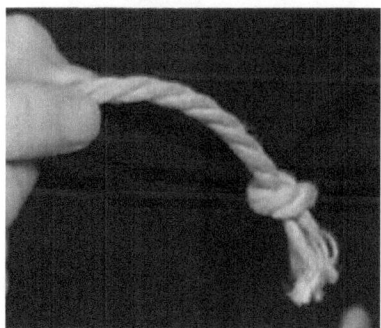

It is not as hard and flattened if you squeeze it, whereas a tightly laid one will not. So, it is a trade-off between flexibility on the one hand and durability on the other. Of course, it does not flow through your hands nicely, and the knots do not compress quite as much, but you are getting a long life in return.

The other thing that varies between different ropes is the yarn count; in other words, how many yarns make up a given rope. The fewer yarns you have, the thicker those yarns will have to be, and this one only had three thick bundles of yarn.

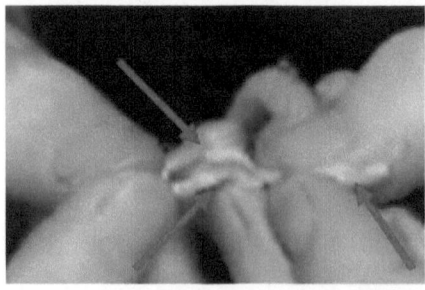

Now, if you take it to the other extreme and count how many we can get.

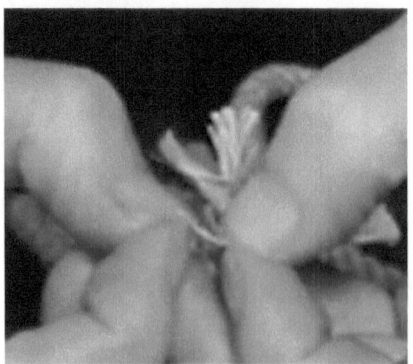

In each of the three, we have seven bundles of yarn. That is not just yarns twisted together; when you carefully unpick them, you will discover five twisted yarns inside each. So you've got five times seven in each of these three plies. So you have three times seven times five; that is your number of yarns. It is a much finer rope, so it feels smoother running through your hands. If you have a low number of yarns, it can feel somewhat abrasive, depending on the construction. But by using so many tiny yarns, we get a fabulous finish.

A similar thing happens with linen hemp; you can see many individual yarns with over 80 yarns in them. That gives a very smooth feel and a clearly defined rope. That is a little bit about yarn count.

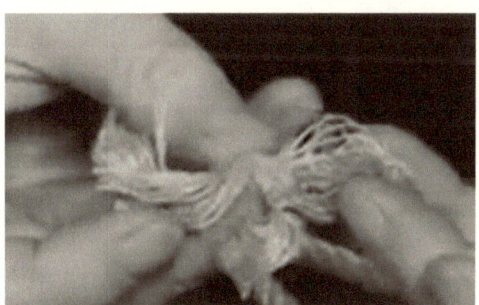

You will come across single or double yarn, so a single yarn is what it sounds like: one bundle of fibers twisted together. A double yarn will be two twisted together.

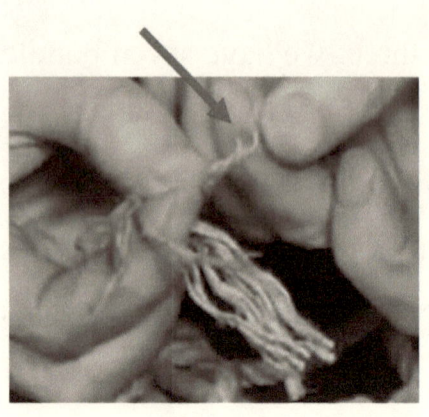

Generally, single yarn ropes will be much finer and smoother because a more significant number of thin yarns allow them to melt together. And that is why this rope with the seven bundles of five yarns is incredibly smooth. Sometimes, double yarn rope can be a little bit less soft. However, the upside is that it tends to be much more stable because you have the double yarn counter twist, which is twisted against the way the rest of the rope works. So they are balancing out against each other. The problem with single yarn is that, as lovely as it is to use, you cannot get the odd yarn working out in a loop after some use. They tend to be looser, with a more gentle twist, making them slightly less resilient. You can get high stranding. High stranding is where you accidentally catch one of these with your finger and pull.

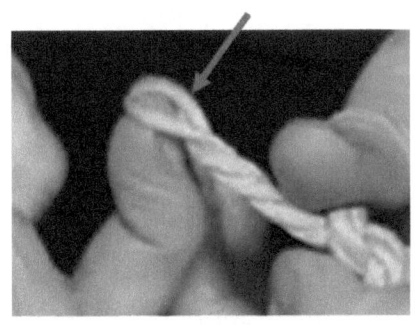 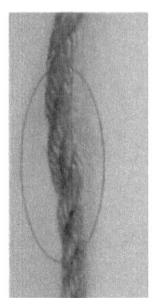

The other thing is that it will create an imbalance, which we call a high strand. And you need to keep on top of those; if you see something like that happening, you need to try and rebalance the rope and work that high strand out to the end of the rope. If you ignore it, it will get worse and get to such a stage where you will not be able to do anything with it, and you just have to throw the rope away.

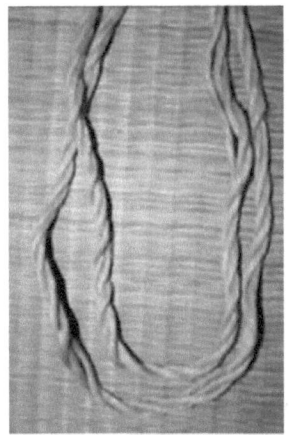

So that is something you need to be conscious of. Several professionals have developed this multi-strand version because we get the benefits of the twists balancing each other out. But because the arms are delicate, they remain very smooth and consistent.

The primary way of differentiating them is like saying that hemp is the sort of broad sword, whereas jute is the rapier. In other words, hemp has a bit of weight. It has a heft when moving the rope; you tend to throw it around slowly and use the weight to carry it. Whereas with jute, you can just literally flick it.

For beginners, you want to look at a rope that will not require massive maintenance to stop high stranding and imbalances. Also, you want a rope that will survive somewhat clumsy handling because it will take a while to master it.

If you are washing rope, always dry it under tension and do not stick it through a drying cycle, particularly not with conditioner, unless you want to fluff up and become stretchy. It is not an excellent way to treat it.

You will find that the loosest ropes tend to, with a bit of use and once they are broken in, open up quite quickly. All you will do is exacerbate that and probably not gain much flexibility and softness.

Another good option for beginners and also for intermediate and advanced riggers, a new asset is an excellent choice.

No loose rope will survive when you catch your finger in it and pull it all. The other thing that is not good is seeing a kink in the rope; try not to pull it out because that is another way of introducing imbalances and causing high stranding. If you see kinks in your rope, gently untwist the kink. Do not get lazy and wrench it out; you will only damage it.

Recommendation on the types of ropes to use

❖ **Nylon rope:**

There is not much problem with nylon ropes. However, you need to ensure that it is braided, not twisted. The downside to nylon ropes is that it is slippery. That is part of what makes it feel nice against the skin. Also, it does not hold knots as you would like. Whenever you do bondage with nylon, make sure to put a couple of extra security knots in place to ensure that it will not loosen or have excess friction. Nylon ropes are great for uplines for suspension work because they are incredibly strong. It will be the line of work that bears multiple weights when doing suspensions. Nylon ropes can bite into the skin and not be the most comfortable. They are good when you do intricate finger or toe bondages. The thin ones are not the best for just regular everyday wrist tying.

❖ Cotton rope:

This rope is very popular, soft, and often dyed in beautiful colors. Some cotton rope might not be quite as soft. When you want to buy it, ensure it has no stiff core. Play around with the rope and make sure that it is soft. Some cotton rope has a stiff core because it is meant for clotheslines. It is not going to work for bondage. You could dye the soft cotton rope or cut it into the needed length. You can also finish the hands of the rope with tread so that they do not come unraveled. The downside to cotton rope is that it has some stretch to it. It is not appropriate for suspension work because of that stretch. Another downside is that knots can get tied into the cotton. Because of the stretch, the knots will tighten significantly, making it inappropriate for suspension work. You can have difficulty getting knots out of cotton because of its propensity to become very heavily knotted. Most forms of bondage, especially when there is a suspension or where the bottom will struggle, are inappropriate.

❖ Jute ropes:

There are a couple of types of jute ropes. They can be beautifully made and conditioned.

❖ **Serenity rope:**

It comes in thick and thin sizes. They can be dyed into any color.

❖ **Hemp rope:**

Hemp is almost the same as jute. The main difference is that hemp is slightly heavier than jute. The good thing about using jute when you tie is that it has teeth. They are natural fibers, so they are grippy. However, they are going to be able to grip each other. You can do friction with the jute and hemp that will hold it in place, but you cannot do the same with nylon ropes. Also, if you have a grass allergy, there is a good chance you will be allergic to jute or hemp. Be aware of that. Rub it against your skin before buying. If you get a reaction, then it may not be for you. You can also run this rub over the skin as much as possible and as quickly as you want. You would still be less likely to have a rope burn. Jute and hemp do not cause rope burning.

Buying jute or hemp for bondage can be very expensive. These groups are generally handspun. They are also appropriately treated with natural oils. The smell of the rope depends on what it is treated with. Because they are natural ropes, they absorb oil and sweat from the skin. Hang or spread them out afterward to dry.

Recommendation on the types of ropes not to use

❖ **Coconut rope:**

This type of rope is scratchy. It splinters into the skin. The initial rope bondage application, coconut rope, is a no! However, you could use it if you are using it with the intent of doing torture ties, causing discomfort to the bottom, and you want it to be scratchy and dig into the skin to splinter. Coconut rope is popular for that sort of thing. Please do not use it for your Shibari rope bondage. It is not generally used for typical bondage but as an accent piece to web across the skin to add to the bondage. This rope is very uncomfortable. Staying away from coconut rope is advisable, especially if you are starting.

❖ **Poly rope:**

It is a stiff plastic terrible rope. It often comes in bright colors like yellow, red, and blue. If you try to tie a knot with a poly rope, it will not hold the knot. Not only will it not hold a knot, but it will also not hold friction. The downside to this rope is that it feels terrible on the skin, is scratchy, and does not hold friction well. It is because it is so stiff, and the heat wants to get all over the place. Do not buy this kind of rope for a Shibari tie.

❖ Sisal rope:

This rope is harsh and scratchy. It splinters and leaves bits of rope in the bottom skin. You do not want this from your rope at all. Avoid this kind of rope. Coconut and sisal ropes may be a natural fiber, but it does not mean it is appropriate for bondage.

Single vs. Double-Ply Ropes

There are single- and double-ply varieties of Shibari ropes. Single-ply ropes are made from a single strand and give smoothness in contrast to double-ply ropes, which have two twisted strands and provide a little more structure and durability. Double-ply ropes are typically chosen for suspension because of their strength.

Depending on the patterns and ties, a different amount of rope will be required. Some ties benefit from softer, more flexible ropes, but others may need tighter ropes for better control. Jute and cotton ropes are well-liked choices, and each has certain characteristics that affect how well they complement various ties.

More about the Ropes and Knots

Symbolism and Expression: Ties That Speak

Each knot has a significant meaning in the world of Shibari. These bonds communicate trust, needs, and feelings in a way that goes beyond the physical. You establish a special connection by communicating feelings that words might find difficult to communicate through this nonverbal language.

Every bend and twist of the rope acts as a stroke of paint on the picture that is your relationship. These intricate connections tell a tale of shared exploration, love, and vulnerability. The things you do not say reveal the depth of your relationship.

⊥ Rope Handling and Ease of Knotting

Effective tying requires careful rope handling. A nicer tying experience is made possible by simple ropes to grip and knot. Jute ropes are well-liked for Shibari because of their all-natural texture and grip, which makes them perfect for firmly holding knots.

⊥ Quality and Material

Shibari-specific ropes are frequently selected because of their consistent quality and traits. Jute, a natural fiber, offers a classic appearance, while nylon, a synthetic fiber, offers strength and flexibility.

⊥ Personal Preference

Shibari fans could have penchants for the rope's feel, texture, and thickness. Finding a rope that suits a practitioner's technique and comfort requires experimentation with various ropes.

To ensure both safety and creative expression, the selection of ropes in Shibari ultimately involves striking a balance between personal preference, tying requirements, and the intended aesthetic.

Impact of Rope Characteristics on Tying Experience

Whether in Shibari or other circumstances, the features of the rope have a considerable impact on the experience of tying:

↓ Influence of Rope Texture on Sensation

The rope's texture influences the sensation of touch during tying. Rougher textures can arouse stronger feelings, enhancing the experience's sensory components.

↓ How Rope Flexibility Affects Tying Techniques

Rope flexibility affects how easily it can be manipulated and knotted. Less flexible ropes may offer better control in some techniques, while supple ropes may simplify tying complex knots and creating desirable patterns.

↓ Exploring Different Rope Diameters for Variability

Rope diameter has a direct effect on the appearance and feel of ties. While thinner ropes produce sharper sensations, thicker ropes may disperse pressure more evenly. Practitioners can customize ties to desired sensations and aesthetics by experimenting with different diameters.

⊥ Rope Material and Construction

The sensation of tying is further influenced by the diverse textures and flexibilities offered by natural fibers like jute and synthetic materials like nylon.

⊥ Balancing Preferences

Practitioners must balance their intended feelings, aesthetics, and skills while choosing a rope's features. A mutually gratifying encounter is ensured via communication between lovers.

To produce the desired aesthetic and sensuous effects in Shibari, one must thoroughly understand how the qualities of the rope combine with tying methods, feelings, and preferences.

⊥ Emphasizing Rope Maintenance for Safety and Longevity

Maintaining rope safety and longevity involves several crucial steps

❖ Importance of Regular Rope Inspection

Conducting routine inspections to find any potential wear, damage, or weaknesses is crucial. Accidents are avoided, and rope longevity is increased with this proactive strategy.

❖ Identifying Signs of Wear and Damage

Examine the fabric for imperfections like fraying, broken strands, flattened regions, and discolorations. These problems may affect the integrity of the rope.

❖ Addressing Frayed Ends and Broken Fibers

Trim broken strands and frayed ends right once to stop further deterioration. Frayed parts can decrease the rope's overall strength.

❖ Lubrication and Moisture Control

Rope lubrication lowers wear and friction. Controlling moisture helps avoid decay and corrosion, particularly in outdoor and marine environments.

❖ Rope Material Matters

Different materials need to be handled differently. Jute and other natural fibers may require extra care to avoid mold, while UV protection is advantageous for synthetic ropes.

❖ Regular Maintenance Schedule

Establish a maintenance program and follow it religiously. Keep track of all maintenance and inspections.

You may increase the longevity and safety of ropes by prioritizing routine inspections, taking early action to address wear and damage, and adhering to recommended maintenance procedures. This will make various applications, such as climbing and rigging, safer and more pleasurable.

❖ Proper Care Techniques for Extending Rope Life

The life of ropes can be significantly increased using the right maintenance methods.

Cleaning Methods and Rope Storage
⬥ Washing and Drying

After use, clean the ropes to remove any dirt or debris that could cause abrasion. Wash gently with a moderate soap and water, then ensure everything is completely dry to avoid mold and mildew.

♣ Coiling, Hanging, or Bundling

Ropes should be kept in a place that is ventilated, dry, and cool. Coiling prevents kinks while hanging or bundling reduces contact with objects that may cause friction or harm.

♣ Protecting Ropes from Sunlight and Extreme Temperatures

Refrain from exposing ropes to intense heat and sunshine, which can weaken the strands and cause degeneration.

♣ Material-Specific Care

Several styles of rope need to be handled differently. For instance, it's important to keep climbing ropes away from harsh substances and cutting edges.

♣ Regular Inspection

Check your ropes frequently for wear, fraying, or other damage. Any rope with deteriorated structural integrity should be replaced. By using the right maintenance procedures, you can extend the life of your ropes while also ensuring their dependability and safety for use in various situations, including general use, rigging, and climbing.

⊥ Ensuring Safety through Rope Maintenance

Ensuring safety during rope use involves several key maintenance practices

❖ Preventing Abrasion and Chaffing

Keep ropes away from chafing against uneven, jagged, or abrasive surfaces. To prevent deterioration and wear, use rope protectors.

❖ Minimizing the Risk of Knot Slippage

To guarantee that your knots are secure, tie them correctly. Consider which knots are best for the job because some are more likely to slip than others.

❖ Storing Ropes in a Tangle-Free Manner

Ropes should be carefully coiled to avoid tangles and knots during storage. A tight bend or kink might cause the rope's integrity to deteriorate.

❖ Regular Inspection

Check your ropes frequently for wear, fraying, or other damage. Any rope with deteriorated solidity should be replaced.

❖ Proper Handling and Techniques

Use ropes properly to minimize stress, friction, and jarring forces that could lead to rope breakdown.

You may increase the safety of using ropes, increase the ropes' lifespan, and avoid accidents by adhering to these maintenance procedures.

Chapter Four

Taking Care of the Ropes

And the better care you take of your ropes, the longer they will last. Of course, they will not last forever; hemp, jute, and organics have a higher tendency to last. However, the longer you use them, the more comfortable they become. They may be coarse at first, but as you use them repeatedly, they become softer cotton and remain soft. However, it will fray, and it will tear apart sooner. Synthetic fibers are the Twinkies of rope that will last forever through nuclear fallout as long as you take care of them and sanitize them.

After playing with the ropes, it is essential to store them properly. Some need to be washed, and others are okay to be used again.

One of the best ways to do this is to create a little loop like

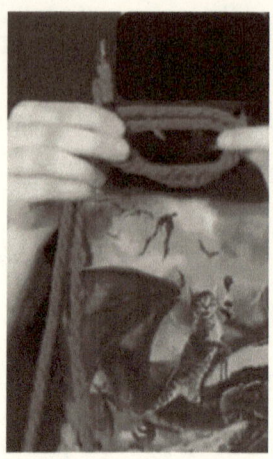

Then, reach inside and pull out the rope.

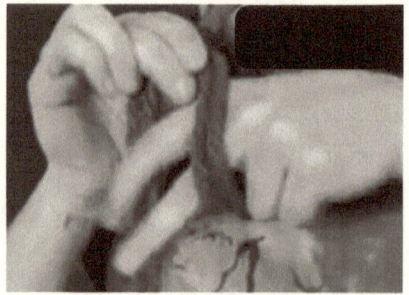

Go on and create another little loop.

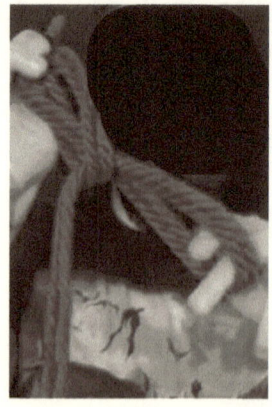

Reach inside that, create another little loop, and keep daisy chaining until you've gone through the entirety of the rope.

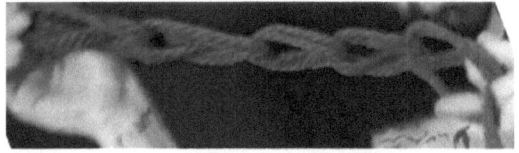

Pull the rope through and taut the last little loop once you are at the end of your rope.

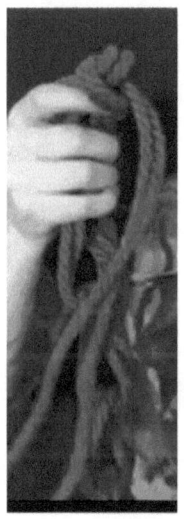

All you have to do now is grab a pillowcase, put the rope inside it, and put it in the wash and a delicate setting. Afterward, unbundle it and let it air dry.

It is essential to remove the cotton rope from the daisy chain. Pull the end of the rope to undo it and have it uncoiled. Be sure to put it into a sink with cold water and wash it with disinfectant spray or soap. Afterward, hang it up to dry.

Nylon ropes are one of the easiest ones to clean. Spray your preferred disinfectant into a rag and start pulling the rope through. Once you have gone through the entirety of the rope, be sure to respray the rag and repeat the process of cleaning it around two to three times. And that is how you clean and take care of your ropes.

Chapter Five

General Rope Bondage Safety

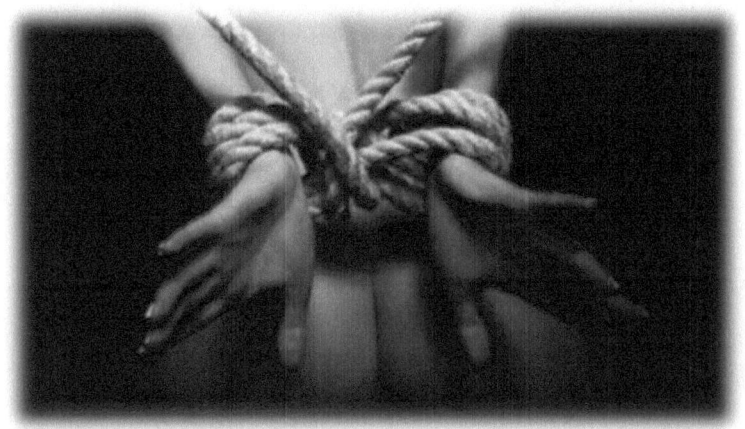

This chapter will introduce all relevant safety aspects you should know about before starting with Shibari and rope bondage. The content will include,

- ➢ rope materials
- ➢ cutting tools
- ➢ self-reflection
- ➢ general safety advice
- ➢ Concrete anatomical safety advice
- ➢ personal risk profile and how to communicate it
- ➢ consent and communication
- ➢ Pain and pain processing strategies
- ➢ psychological aspects and TRE

Rope bondage can come with a variety of potential risks and damages. Therefore, we consider it a recreational activity, which means whisking away a consensual kink.

To enable safe and satisfying experiences with rope bondage, we want to empower you to know, assess, and control all potential risks. Only by full consciousness can you act and play consensual.

Rope materials

When you start with rope bondage, one of the most asked questions is, which rope material is the most suitable for you? We can divide rope materials into natural and synthetic fibers.

Cutting tools

You should have a cutting tool from the first bondage scene you are doing. But you should not only have it in your bag but also have it ready and handy. It might sound trivial to train how to use a cutting tool. However, in an emergency, you might get panic and tunnel vision, and things you do confidently in your daily life might get complicated. So train with your cutting tool. For instance, a knife without a hidden blade can easily harm your partner because you can accidentally cut into someone's flesh. So, such knives are not suitable for use as cutting tools. Medical scissors are safe for cutting tools because they have a rounded edge.

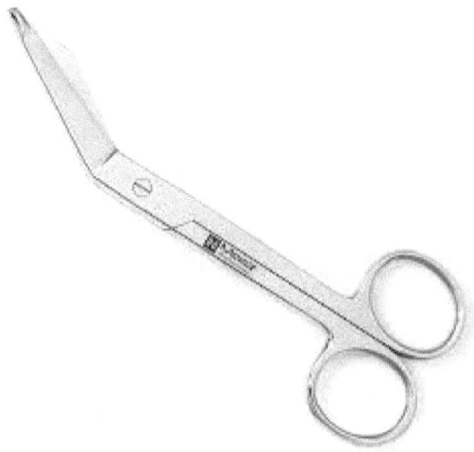

They also have a hidden blade because of that rounded edge. But the blade is slippery and will not cut the rope easily. so this might be an option to cut your rope. After you have used it once, it will get stumped, and you will have changed the cutting tool.

Another option as a cutting tool is a textile scissor. A textile scissor also has a rounded edge, so it will be safe to use on someone's body, and the blade is jacked, so it is easier to cut into the ropes.

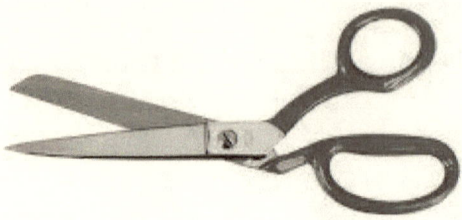

The blade is jacked, and you will have an excellent grip when cutting a rope. However, you can use it up to three times and will get stumped, too, and you will have to buy another one.

Rescue and belt cutters are also excellent cutting tool options because they have a rounded edge and are sharp, like razor blades. There are different versions of rescue and belt cutters; they are both suitable for cutting tools. The good thing about using that tool is that you do not have to change the whole device after using it once; you can only change the blades and keep the tools. So, this is very suitable to use as a cutting tool for rope.

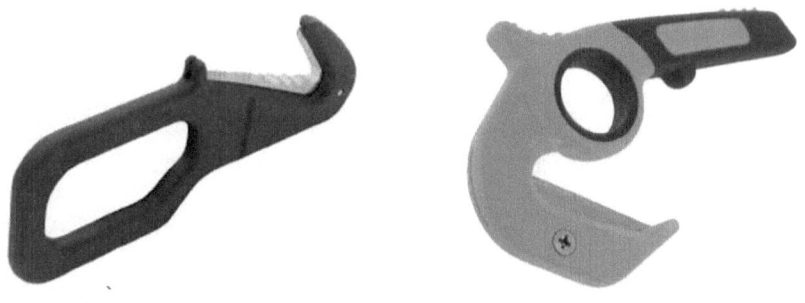

If you have chosen a cutting tool, you should try it at home. For example, you should buy three or more if you use a scissor as a cutting tool. After trying it out, you will need a new one for your bondage scene, and when you have used it once, it will be stumped, and you will need a new one, so buy more than one. If you decide to use a rescue belt cutter, purchase new blades to change them after you use them.

X   ✓

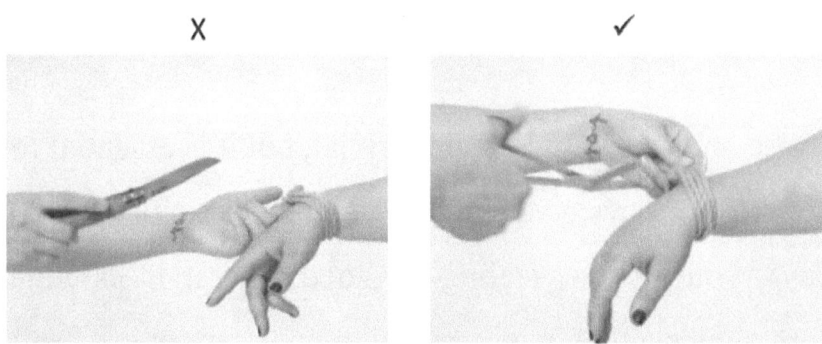

General safety advice

There is some general safety advice list you should always check whenever you tie in with a person.

If you want to tie or get tied by someone for the first time, please inform yourself about the person before starting to tie. You can read the internet profile, ask friends in your local community, and please do not get dazzled by fame, representative pictures, or names. Before starting a rope scene with someone, consider a few things.

The general safety checklist contains the following points,

➢ Check your rope equipment every time you use it.
➢ Check the suspension point every time you want to use it.
➢ Have you slept enough?
➢ Have you eaten and drank enough?
➢ Do you feel emotionally and physically ready to tie and get tied?

These questions might sound trivial, but it is essential to ask them. Some days, you feel better about getting tied, and some days, you are not feeling so good, and it is essential to communicate that in advance with your partner.

Another question is, have you consumed any drugs? You should not do rope bondage if you are under the influence of any drugs,

> Have you taken any medication?

> Have you discussed your limits and expectations?

> Are you informed about the potential risks?

> Have you communicated about pre-existing diseases? Especially asthma, diabetes, and epilepsy are diseases you should speak about in advance. And suppose you have any emergency medications like tablets or an inhaler. In that case, you should have it in your bag and ready and handy, which is the most critical point.

Educate your partner on how to use your medication because when tied up and need your inhaler, it will be vital that your partner knows how to handle it.

Anatomy, nerves, and fainting

Nerves and nerve damage are the highest risks when doing rope bondage. The risk of getting injured by rope bondage is relatively high compared to other kinks. Some of these injuries are not noteworthy from a medical point of view but maybe from a personal point of view. They include,

> hematoma

> rope burn

> rope marks

- petechia and
- blister

You might get blue marks as you lay your body weight in ropes. The risk increases with suspension and depends on your sensitivity. Rope burn can quickly arise by pulling the rope too fast over your skin. Rope marks usually disappear after a few hours and show the pressure marks where the rope has been on your body. Petechia are lots of small glue spots that look like freckles that often arise on your arm when there has been high tension on the ropes. It may be due to some small capillary vessels bursting under stress to create these small blue dots. Blisters can occur due to high pressure on your body, and water gets pressed out of your cells. It is the same procedure as when you are getting blisters on your feet.

More severe injuries are, foremost, nerve damage and, secondly, fainting. Getting nerve damage through rope bondage is the most popular and formidable injury. Most everyone doing rope bondage will experience nerve damage symptoms sooner or later or even get injured. There is no way to purge the risk thoroughly, but many ways exist to decrease it.

It is impossible to tie someone without crossing through nerves; they are everywhere in our bodies.

In bondage, we are usually affected by nerve damage in the arms, which is a massive problem for most people in their daily lives when their hands are handicapped. Enough damage, in the case of rope tying, is damage caused by compression. That means the nerve was compressed too long and hard, and the myelin was damaged.

Damaged myelin cannot guarantee fast and entire signal forwarding anymore. Depending on whether the injured nerve is a motor or sensory one, you will have symptoms of asthenia. That means you have decreased muscle power or symptoms of sensory loss. A pending nerve injury does not come along with painful symptoms. It can even come without any symptoms; the first symptoms you notice will already be a loss of motor or sensory skills. Your only possibility to decrease the risk is to know about potentially dangerous areas to tie on and know about hand function tests.

Potential dangerous areas

Although it might be possible to get nerve damage in your legs or feet, the potential risk is lower than getting a nerve injury in your arms.

Three major nerves innervate the arm, so all have their source in the spine: radial, median, and ulnar. They all have their origin in the spine, moving down the neck to the armpit with the same course to that point of the armpit called plexus brachialis. After that point, the nerves will have different approaches. For example, the median nerve has its system straight down the middle of the upper arm and forearm. The ulnar nerve takes the same path here at the upper arm, but then at the forearm, it moves down at the site of the pinky finger. Finally, the radial nerve has a relatively more intricate course. It has the same approach in the upper arm. But somewhere underneath half of the upper arm, it turns outwards and moves down your forearm to the side of your thumb. Somewhere underneath the half of the upper arm, the radial nerve will turn out, move around your elbow, and then down at the side of your thumb down the forearm.

One potential risk area is around the wrists. All three nerves are superficial in this part of your arm, so it is easy to harm them. You have to consider that when tying handcuffs. Another potential risk area is inside your upper arm because all three nerves run through that point.

If you put the arm close to your body, the rope will run through the body and arms; there can be a pressure point by the rope which compresses the nerves inside the upper arm. So, this is also a potential risk area to keep in mind. The last potential risk area is here at your plexus brachialis in your armpit.

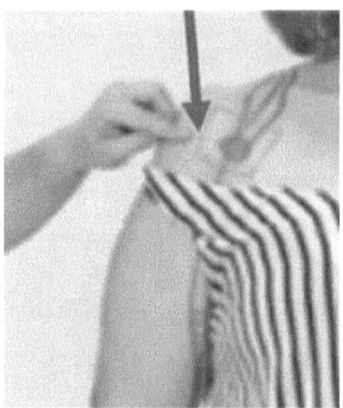

That might be a potential risk when tying chest harnesses or neck ropes because a neck rope and tension can create too much pressure on all three nerves running through your neck into your armpit. It can cause temporary paralysis of the arm. So, your potential risk areas are the armpit, the inner side of your upper arm, and your wrists.

Another potential risk area might be the outside of your upper arm, especially when your arms are in the TK position.

Some of the already many potential risk areas, like the wrists, are still visible. But at your upper arm, you will not see that many dangerous regions on the outside. It is because you can see the turn of the radial nerve outside the arm or the lower half of the upper arm. It depends on your anatomy where it turns to the outside. So when you are tying it TK, an advanced pattern, you should train for it. You might tie above the radial nerve while tying in the TK position. Tying every small in the upper half of your arm may be advisable to stay safe in case of nerve damage.

In your arm's lower half, your radial nerve turns to the outside; this is another potential risk area, and you should remember that.

If you start practicing, you will soon recognize that it is impossible to tie someone without tying on some risky areas.

Therefore, there is no need to keep them fully untied. However, there is a need to tie it with special attention. Use a flat rope with no torsion, no knots on potential pressure points, and good tension.

You can check the function of your hands by using the following techniques,

➢ giving a thumbs up,
➢ pressing your wrist backward on the upper side of your forearm,
➢ clenching fists, opening,
➢ closing your hands and
➢ touching every finger with your thumb to check your sensitivity.

The essential checks to the radial nerve are thumbs up and pressing your wrist backward. If you are not handicapped in doing any of the abovementioned things, your motor skills are excellent.

Please decide how often you want to do your hands check and if you want to do it on your own or if you want to do it by request of your rigger. A sensory symptom of nerve damage can be tingling in single fingers. For example, thumb and index finger tingling indicates sensory loss of your radial nerve, but your motor skills can still be fine. So tingling in single fingers should always be communicated because it is sure enough damage symptom. Tingling in your whole hand is mostly a symptom of blood stasis. It is a normal physical reaction, and the blood stasis is medically not noteworthy if you do not keep it for one whole day. Doing your hand checks might be a problem because you cannot notice when a single finger tingles if your full hand tingles. You can only check your motor skills.

Decide how you want to deal with sensitivity loss in your hand due to blood stasis with your partner. That is a fundamental question to discuss in advance. The most common nerve damage is the so-called falling hand, where your wrist cannot bend backward anymore. For example, you cannot give a thumbs up or move your wrist back. The injured nerve is your radial nerve. It might be that you will be fully recovered after a few hours, but days or weeks might also be needed to recover.

As a rule of thumb, the longer the compression has endured, the longer the nerve damage will last. The sooner you recognize a problem, the sooner you relieve the compression, and the sooner you will recover. And so carry out checks regularly during your tying scene. Communicate if you recognize any problem or feel insecure about the status of their nerves.

If you have nerve damage, do not feel guilty, and please avoid any form of further compression. Do not massage or tie if the injury is present. Instead, care for each other, talk about the injury, and how you feel about that damage. Avoid randomly taking painkillers because no medication helps a nerve recover faster.

If you do not feel pain, you usually do not have pain when you have nerve damage; do not take painkillers. If you feel safe about it, visit your doctor and tell him honestly what happened so the doctor can check the degree of nerve damage.

An essential piece of advice is to be patient. That is the hardest but the best treatment to recover your nerve damage.

Fainting can have many causes;

- warm temperature,
- standing for a long time,
- an abrupt change from standing to sitting or from sitting to standing,
- dehydration,
- leukemia,
- wrong breathing,
- strong pain stimuli or nervous-stimulated fainting.

If you notice these feelings, getting nauseous or cold sweat, you may feel tingling in your ears before fainting. You will have enough time to communicate that you feel bad and want to get down to the floor as fast as possible. It helps if you focus on breathing in through your nose slowly but deeply and breathing out strongly through your compressed lips.

As a rigger, be aware that when bringing the tied person back to the floor, in case the person faints. It might be helpful to speak with each other. As a rigger, talk to your partner calmly and constantly and bring them down as fast as possible.

Nerval-stimulated fainting works a little differently. Mostly, the solar plexus causes it. The solar plexus is a nervous structure between your sternum and your belly. Intense pressure in this area can cause fainting due to nervous reactions that influence blood pressure regulation. As a result, you will feel nauseous very fast and may not have time to communicate that you have started fainting.

You can also faint by compressing the carotid sinus, a neural structure at your neck. We highly recommend not to play any neckrope before you are a routine rigger. Fainting due to a carotid sinus nervous reaction will happen in less than a few seconds; you may not be able to communicate anything before you faint.

In handling these situations, it does not matter what the cause of fainting is; the first aid measures are always the same. The first aid measures are to stay calm, stay focused, talk to your partner, and bring your partner down to the floor as fast as possible but without any panic. Lay them on the back and put the legs up on a chair to help their circulation to improve. If they are gagged or blindfolded, remove that immediately and observe them.

Usually, the person should wake up after a few seconds. It might be that they feel a little disorientated or overwhelmed. Be calm, talk to them, and help them return to orientation.

Untying is the last priority; unless you have the rope around the neck or the face, you should cut it immediately.

Personal risk profile

The responsibility in rope bondage is always shared. Those participating partners should be responsible for themselves and their partners. Both communicate the limits, statutes, and readiness to assume risk. It might be worth a great session to condone nerve damage for some people. But for others, it might be the biggest fear of getting nerve damage. That is why having a personal risk profile and sharing it with your partner is so important. We recommend that the shape was the lower readiness to assume risk; it always should be the one that guides you. Remember, "a chain is only as strong as its weakest link,"

Some of these questions can help you with creating a personal risk profile.

1. What are your experiences in rigging in modeling, first-aid, blood stasis, and nerve damage?
2. Are there any ties you do not want, or are you feeling insecure? Communicate about that

3. Do you want suspension, and if you are going to do suspension, do you want to do static or dynamic poses?

4. Do you want a time limitation for your time being suspended?

5. It is crucial to check your hand function, self-determined or by request of your rigger. It would help if you communicated that in advance of your session.

6. How frequently do you want your hands checked, or check your hands on your own?

7. What and how do you want to communicate during the process of tying? For example, do you want constant feedback? Do you want to communicate verbally or nonverbal? Do you like to share during and after the session or at specific times?

8. How do you wish to deal with tingling sensations, maybe in your hands?

9. Do you have special anatomical needs like slipped discs, artificial joints, or implants? Communicate that in advance because maybe you have to adapt your ties.

10. As a model, is there any psychological trauma that might arise when you are tied? And if you are in subspace, can

you still monitor yourself and your hand functions? Think about that in advance.

Consent and communication

Most consent violations do not happen because someone decided intentionally to harm somebody else but because of misunderstanding and miscommunication. Therefore, straightforward and concrete prior communication about boundaries is essential. In contrast, negotiation is the establishment of certain limits and safe words. Option in negotiation means that only the activities discussed and agreed to are part of a play. Otherwise, anything is fair game except the hard limits or activities deemed off-limits.

Consensual, non-consent is typically a relationship style, but some people play within this structure. In this style, the person in authority makes the decisions, and the person giving up their power obeys even if they do not want to. It is advisable to establish extensive and detailed content negotiation before a session of interaction starts between everyone involved. in this negotiation. We share things we consent to and the same with our partners. A point someone does not want to be concerned about can be discussed, and a middle ground can often be found. It is not coercion, not a tit-for-tat exchange; it is a mutual discovery of where everyone overlaps in their desires.

Have you shared your risk profile and thought about your preferred communication style? Reflect on your role. It is a common misbelief that one tying plays the active part, and the one getting tied plays the passive part. But, both partnered to participate in a bondage scene actively; nobody is the passive sense of motionless condoning. The one who gets tied shapes are seen by their reactions, body tension, and movement. And sometimes, the one who gets tied proactively asks a rigger to do a specific position on them. In such a situation, the one who gets tied is not the one who is in a receiving role. But most people would assume the rigger as giving or taking and the one getting tied as the one who is allowing or receiving.

Think about your preferred setting. For example, do you want to publicly or privately tie a session or training mode? Do you want to use a safe word or a traffic light code? Do you want time limitations on how long you want to be suspended? How long do you want to be in a tie, and do you want to have some test tying, like three minutes of floor work with only one rope?

Traffic light coats mean you have green, yellow, and red colors. If you are using green, you are all right with the situation. However, if you are using yellow, you came close to your limits but did not want the scene to stop. Instead, you want to slow down the scene. If you use red, you have crossed your limits and want the scene to stop immediately.

How do you feel about blindfolds and gags? Do you want any no-rope-related toys or activities, and what do you think about nudity? How and where do or do you not want to get touched?

Do you want to get dominated, or do you want to dominate someone while tying?

These questions might sound trivial, but bondage and BDSM can be separate categories or belong together. Furthermore, people have very different intentions regarding what they seek in rope bondage.

Pain processing strategies

A frequently asked question in rope bondage is whether you know if something is bad or good pain. It sounds like a complicated question, but in the end, it is not that complicated. Your body is much more independent from your ratio than you might think, and it knows on its own what is good and bad pain.

First of all, pain is always only in information. So, your body wants to be aware of the coming sensation. But suppose that pain sends information that there is a danger, and the potential injury might arise. In that case, your body will react knee-jerkingly. There will be an adrenaline standard. You will feel panic, and your muscles will defend and increase tension. You immediately want to escape the situation. That kind of pain and pain processing is always a kind of bad pain. So when you feel pain and panic, you should always change the tie immediately or untie it and escape the situation.

But suppose there is pain information that makes you feel discomfort, itching, biting, or pressing. In that case, it is just information to keep observing the situation. Your body wants to tell you you should monitor the status and the pain, but it is unnecessary for a knee-jerking reaction. That is only to make you aware there might be danger potentially doing the situation. So, in this painful situation, you can decide on your own whether you want to stand that pain or not and for how long. Sometimes, it is necessary to tell your partner where it hurts, how it hurts, and how long you can stand or want to. But it is a conscious decision you can take on your own. This kind of pain is what we can call good pain or potentially good pain. It depends on you whether this is good pain or not, but it is not life-threatening or not a sign of a potential injury. So it is not bad pain. You can use breathing techniques to improve the situation in this painful situation. Breathe slowly and deeply through your nose for four seconds, hold your breaths for seven seconds, and breathe out slowly and deeply for eight seconds. Suppose you repeat that three times; you will be astonished at how relaxed and calm your body will become. And this can be an excellent strategy for dealing with pain.

Another pain processing strategy is tongue relaxation. Your tongue and mouth are connected to your whole body. So if your tongue is tensed, your whole body is tensed, but if you start relaxing your tongue actively, you relax. The more comfortable you are, the easier it will be to stand the situation. so do not try to overthink what is good or bad pain. Your body already knows about that. If you can decide whether it's good or bad pain, it will be potentially good pain because you have time to decide. But it will be a bad pain if you must escape very soon.

Psychological aspects and T.R.E

TRE means trauma and tension release exercises. So, being tied up and experiencing a situation of being helpless and dependent on the other person might put you in a headspace where all the experiences of your biography or even trauma might come up. You can compare it a little bit with a headspace of being hypnotized. While in that headspace, you can quickly enter parts of your soul you haven't seen or recognized for a long time. That can be a very positive experience but also a scary one.

Experiencing injuries can also be very scary; no matter how deeply you have been informed on a theoretical base, you will be frightened if your practical experience is practical.

Therefore, the experience of an injury through bondage might be a traumatic or frightening experience for you.

Having a tying party with whom you can imagine speaking about those feelings and psychological flashbacks is beneficial. Before deciding with whom you tie and what you want to tie, you should ask yourself whether you can imagine having that trust level and talk about these topics. Because then you can decide how deep you want to dive into the tying scene or how scary the stuff should be you will try out. You might experience shivering after you've been getting tight. That is a normal physical reaction that does not necessarily involve being cold. It might have been a natural stress relief mechanism called tension trauma release. Trauma does not necessarily have to be associated negatively. Trauma is any stressful impact that develops into freezing, fainting, or fighting. So, if your body experiences stressful implications, you will start fighting, freezing, or fainting. It will mostly fight in a bonded context because your muscle tension will increase. Maybe at some point, you will find acceptance, your tension relieved, and you will let go. But up to that point, reacting with higher mass tension or freezing or fainting is just a natural process. A relaxation phase will follow after certain muscle groups get stressed and stretched. Many animals react that way, and children naturally respond like that. However, adult humans are too much in control of their bodies to experience this natural stress relief mechanism. You can discover the shivering experience without getting tight by practicing trauma and release exercises. Tension and trauma release exercises are simple yet innovative exercises that assist the body and release deep muscular stress, tension, and trauma patterns. TRE safely activates a natural reflex mechanism of shaking or vibrating, releasing muscular tension from the nervous system.

Consent Advice for Rope Bondage

In Shibari, consent is co-creating, an agreement on creating joy. So, it is not giving or taking, but it is making.

We can all try to teach consent, but it is an ongoing discussion with our partners and the people around us. In the society that we live in, unfortunately, the conversation around consent is a genuine concern because it is a relatively modern phenomenon. So often, the way humans, power, and society happen, consent or mutual agreement of what is to happen has been rare. We are, in many ways, sophisticated and yet in development. So, if you are baffled, internally conflicted, feeling like you do not have enough information, or have made mistakes around consent, be kind to yourself. Consent awareness is a cultural bleeding edge and a new way we think about human interaction.

Consent in our kinky play also influences how we engage with mutuality, agency, and boundaries in everyday life and societal assumptions. For example, some people ask what is so hard about consent if you can agree on a thing as they advance, but if only it were that easy.

When we talk about giving consent, it usually gives the idea that makes it almost seem like there is a thing that you, something that you will offer to a partner. But that can be a wrong way of thinking about it or at least not a helpful way of thinking about it.

Consent is rooted in romantic languages of sensing or feeling together to feel right. So, if you have consent and could either give it or withhold it, that is transactional. It is your consent; your partner needs to persuade it out of you, or you hold it.

Taking and giving consent

So what if we created consent together instead of taking and giving? There is never a diminishment if we do not talk about taking and giving. So you always possess a total capacity to create limitations and agreement, always full capacity. We can do a lot to lay our foundations around consent by noticing how many opportunities for consent creation happen in ordinary life. And what is your habit around actively participating in consent opportunities that involve you and advocating for yourself?

Translate that for a dating and bondage situation; how do you gauge your interests, limits, and boundaries.

As a piece of advice, some practices in Shibari are exciting but do not do everything in the first scene. Instead, allow yourself to do a few things well and give yourself space to reflect upon them.

We often do not know our limits and boundaries until we come up against them, and coming up against them and learning them can be painful. There is no way to avoid them. However, there are ways we can minimize it since we cannot entirely prevent them. So, as a piece of advice, start with simple scenes. If anything feels odd and out of place, think twice about it.

Some people come up against their experience walls, smash into them at full strength, and slide off the boundary. And then stand up, brush themselves off, and go merry.

Other people, coming up against something upsetting or a newly discovered boundary, find it difficult to go on. But, again, it is neither good nor bad; this is just a character, and understand it will vary by life circumstances.

But what type are you? Are you a slam against the wall, brush-up, and carry-on person? Or are you somebody who is profoundly impacted by coming up against boundaries and limits?

Depending on how you deal with unexpected disasters, those who slam up against the wall and figure it out make mistakes and try many things. But if you are sensitive to a deep resonance, take small steps and understand yourself.

In other words, create joy with yourself and your partner, agreement on joy-making, boundaries, and limits. Boundaries and limits are that which take away from collaborative joy-making.

What kind of mood do we want to create? That does not seem like it explicitly is about consent or boundaries. However, everything weaves in. Thinking about limits, boundaries, and consent can seem intimidating if you are new. It is huge. Instead, think about what kind of mood you want. What is the reason for the scene? Did your partner ask you to tie them up in a hogtie? Or is what they are asking about, or do they want to feel like you are taking possession of their body and that they are helpless in your ministrations? It might be that, and instead of saying to tie them.

Naming a position is not identifying a mood. Naming a mood and then saying a position might help, but that is another thing. Image, your partner wants to feel like a bound captive and helpless against your administration. Imagining a hogtie might help her feel that way. It is one way to think about it. So, what does this have to do with consent? We are co-creating, so your mood can inform you and your partner about the genre in which you are not going to. It will make decisions more manageable for both parties; all parties maybe you have more than two in your scene. So think in terms of genre and movie genre mood, think in terms of that, and it will help decision-making.

115

Boundaries and limits are not the same but work well together. Think about boundaries as that which, if we cross into them, will take away from the joy of our experience. In contrast, limits are the specifics that shall not exist because they will create negative consequences.

About the difference between limits and boundaries, many other excellent thinkers around limit consent and boundaries also have overlapping but different ways of looking at this.

Boundaries take away from our joy of the shared experience. Consent means co-creating, an agreement around creating fun. It is not giving or taking but creating. Limit is that which may cause harm. And harm could be significant harm or slight harm. For example, pulling the hair could be harmful but still harmful. Triggering a previous sexual trauma causes substantial harm. Poking on a bruise if told you not to is probably a little harmful. Creating giant marks when appearing in public and having a big handprint on the face causes extensive harm.

Discussion with a new partner
Discuss with a new partner if you do not fully know your limits and hard limits to any scene. Say if you are new to this

and do not know how you will respond to it if you are curious but interested. Maybe you do not see your reactions; you think you will love it or might not, declare that upfront. Also, there is a lot that you do not know about yourself. State upfront that you want to give information, and you will provide the best you can.

Before going into a scene, understand what kind of mood you want. Pay attention if this new partner is paying attention to you. If they are not and do not comprehend what you are saying, consider not playing with them. Just because a person may be awesomely skilled at tying human beings up does not correlate with someone being awesome about communicating, connecting, and giving a damn about another person. It is easy to confuse technical proficiency with human excellence, and it is also easy to hide the lack of human excellence behind technical ability. So it is advisable to play with somebody with excellent human excellence and little to no rope skills and then make them go through all the Shibari's study. That is better than finding somebody who is a shitty human being but has excellent gift-wrapping skills.

Boundary versus Limit

Take note of what would be a boundary for you; outside of this would distract from the feel-good and limit, and if you step into the subsequent territory, it will cause harm.

Tell the other person what you look and sound like when it is good for you and what they will see and hear when it is not. And not good is boring.

If the other person does not know, ask what they look like and sound like when it is good or see when it is not.

If you do not know what a happy face is, here are multiple choices you can ask and give the best guess possible.

➢ Do you think your eyes will be open or closed?
➢ Are you making noise or not noise?
➢ Are you using words, not words?
➢ Are you moving a lot, or are you super still?
➢ What do you look like, or how do you sound?

Those are some excellent places to start with; give some specifics, and you can ask yourself those questions. And if you are not sure, you might have playmates you can ask.

If we are new, we will likely not know so much that is true, but it is worth asking the question because we also may have other data to gather. It helps people take inventory of, think, and feel back to their happy place and start a self-assessment. But, again, the responsibility falls on both you and your partners.

The look-like, sound-like for not good happens before the safe word, including boring. If you are having a not-good, this is heading into the boundary that takes away from the joy; maybe it is just mildly annoying. And if you say safeword, that will only let your partner know when potential harm is about to happen instead of allowing them to continue. For some models, when they start to get to a not-good place, they make a fist. This is not a safe word; this is the model of processing negative discomfort and making fists happen viscerally and bodily well before they can form words.

For a safe word, words are essential, but like an emergency handbrake. Sometimes, for some people. It is the last resort to discomfort or feeling unhappy. So if you can tell your person what you look like, sound like, or not good is, and if your person is paying attention, this goes both ways, then there is an opportunity to change the course of the scene.

Consent is collaborative co-creation for potential joy, so we are making collaboration, not giving or taking.

Sometimes, our partners deny us consent because they are not paying attention. By noticing our opportunities to make consent, even something similar, we are building our consent muscle to recognize when we can make this and when others deny it.

Consent, limits, and boundaries are not a checklist of how to do; it is building a skill set and learning along the way.

Chapter Six

Basic Knots and Techniques

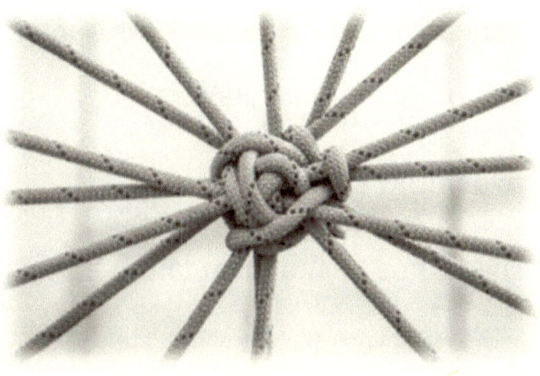

Due to their usefulness and adaptability, foundational knots are essential in various activities and industries. They are essential for efficiency and safety in addition to being functional. Foundational knots hold loads and secure equipment in sailing, climbing, camping, and construction. For instance, the square knot works well for firmly linking two ropes of the same diameter, while the strength and dependability of the bowline knot make it indispensable for constructing loops that do not slip. These knots have been passed down through the years due to their durability and efficacy. Foundational knots offer the stability and strength required to complete tasks securely and successfully, from fastening sails to constructing shelters.

Techniques of Knot Tying

There are many different techniques for tying knots. Some of the most common techniques include:

- **The overhand knot**

The most basic knot is the foundation for numerous other knots.

- **The square knot**

This knot is used to connect two rope segments.

- **The bowline**

This knot is used to make a non-slip loop in a rope.

- **The clove hitch**

This knot is utilized to fasten a rope to anything.

- **The figure eight knot**

This knot is a stopper knot to keep a rope from sliding through an object.

Detailed Instructions on How to Tie Essential Knots

Here are detailed instructions on how to tie four essential knots:

Square knot

Start by creating a loop in the rope using the working end before tying a square knot. Then, form another loop by crossing the working end over the standing end. Tighten the knot after re-looping the working end through the initial loop.

Bowline

Making a loop in the rope with the working end is the first step in tying a bowline. Put the working end through the loop after the standing end. Tighten the knot after bringing the working end back up through the loop.

Clove hitch

Start by creating a loop in the rope with the working end before tying a clove hitch. The working end should be wrapped around the item to which the rope will be fastened before re-looped. Enforce the knot.

Figure eight knot

Making a loop in the rope using the working end is the first step in tying a figure eight knot. Circumambulate the standing end with the working end before returning through the loop. Cinch the knot

Safety Precautions and Troubleshooting in Techniques
When dealing with knots and rope procedures, safety must always come first. Dangerous circumstances might result from improper knot tying. Ensuring sufficient knot security and stability is essential to avoid slippage or failure. Rope burns, falls, and equipment damage are all possible risks. All safety precautions include avoiding stress loading, not overloading rope, and utilizing the right knots for particular activities. Knots coming undone because of poor tying or poor knot choice are typical troubleshooting problems. Ensure knots are tied correctly, and keep up with routine inspections to remedy them. On knot safety, Animated Knots has a wealth of information available. Examples of safety knots can be found in the National Tree Climbing Guide. Remember that the best way to reduce dangers related to

ropes and knots is to prioritize safety through proper procedures, proper knots, and routine inspection.

Chapter Seven

Sensuality in Rope Bondage

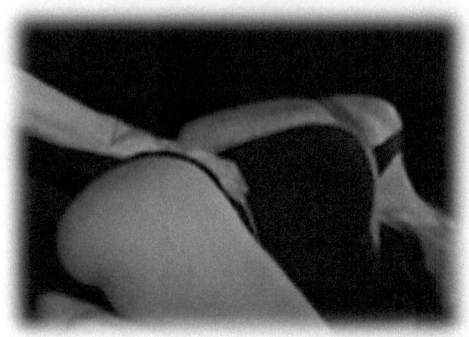

You could view tying as a form of touch, but the difference is that ropes also grip and stay on the body. So, if you consider it this way as a continuous buildup of communication, it should be interesting to ask what quality of touch we give when we tie. What kind of touch and manipulation your partner receives should be very interesting. But not just for organizing as good an experience or engaging an experience as possible for your partner but also for you if you are the rigger. Ensure you are seen in the tying process and express what you intend to communicate through the ropes.

So, Shibari's most sensually powerful trait is the intense focus on each other during the tying process.

Some essential questions may include,

➢ How do I want to be focused on by this person?

➢ What am I willing to accept?

➢ What kind of focus am I willing to accept?

➢ What kind of focus do I want or urging to receive from the person tying me?

➢ What kind of focus am I willing and capable of giving during this session with this person?

When you tie someone, it may be a casual situation, and you do not intend to make it super sexual or super edgy. However, the person tying you focuses on your body when they are tying you. So, no matter the intention, you are highly focused on and observing each other in this heightened state. So you can amplify both emotions and sensational feelings in your body. So transform them like you can view the body of the person being tied.

And it would help if you played with the fact that it is undeniable where your focus is on your partner while you are tying them. You can make this into a playful element. Use it to your advantage because not only the ropes or touch, but the quality of touch is essential in rope, and also gaze like

127

watching. And because we are constantly physically interacting, many curious things are happening and progressing during a tying session. We might not always have eye contact because this focus is still intense. Your partner may not see your face; perhaps they are blindfolded or looking away while you are tying over some other part of their body. But you can still be sure that they are anticipating your gaze. They are feeling your eyes or wondering where you are looking. It is a potent erotic tool.

Consider picking a position exposing itself and how you approach it to make it feel like the person is being observed getting into the role. You can feel it when it is pragmatic and technical and lacks emotion. You can feel the way that the person moves you. It is going to be entirely mechanical. The person will not try to give anything more than what is expected when you are tying something in a very neutral way.

An excellent way to approach Shibari as an essential practice is to view the person's body being tied like a map.

You can view the whole body with its emotional value or function and sensitivity to different types of touch or force.

For example, the waist is sensual and vulnerable for most people. On the other hand, it is soft and pliable; we are rarely touched there except maybe during sex or if we have an intimate hug with a friend. While perhaps in the upper arms, we feel less vulnerable, it is also a place where if you want to hold on to someone strong, this might be the place you choose to grab someone. So, the whole of your body is a detailed map of many different sensations and meanings and additional toughness and softness. And when the rope model, you should be very interested in exploring this and figuring it out. There are some general things you can guess or guess from yourself by evaluating your own body or examining your own body.

Each individual is different; each individual feels differently about various body parts or handles pain worse in some features than others. So see if you notice any particular positive reaction or tense up; maybe they lean and encourage you to go further, or perhaps they get a bit nervous. You can also discuss it before or after a scene to know more. It is not only about the person trying to control and make an experience for the person tied. Also, try to connect with how the model feels. What does a body part or position feel? What do you want to see? Are you allowed to do something and enjoy that you can enjoy and play with the person?

Many shapes that we use are also designed to force the person to be in an erotically appealing or exposing position. For example, suppose you do a tie that spreads the legs. In that case, you can expect your partner to feel the pulling on the legs and a heightened awareness of the area being exposed in the right headspace. Even more so, if they think or guess that someone's eyes are upon them in that area, it will make the person tired and hyper-aware of this place, like the crotch or whatever.

In an intense situation like this of feeling watched, it can feel like you can feel blood pumping or your skin tingling. Do not just continue adding on more and more things but linger at the moment. Try to approach what you are doing with some subtleness and some slowness.

It is all about building up anticipation and building up more and more excitement or arousing energy. Suppose you go straightforward and get what you want or expect directly. In that case, this can cut the fantasy short. Play with the teasing and the buildup. And if you want to play in this way, it is good to consider what could be distracting from the thing you want to be the central theme.

You also must remember that if too many other things compete for attention, the item you are trying to amplify may drown out. And it can be simple little things like a wrist cuff is uneven. It is cutting into the wrists, and it is okay. However, it is still enough of a great sensation to distract from your focus.

Chapter Eight

Tying the Bones and Ropes Hip Harness

Tying single-column ties on a partner's waist can sometimes be tricky, so you have to spend time practicing it.

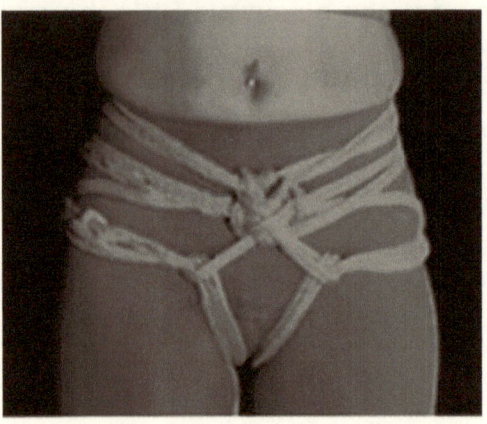

If you find it hard, we often teach another little hack: to go around the waist once and then pinch the rope.

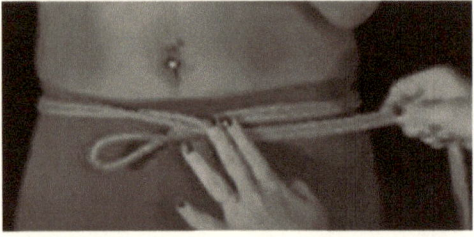

And then you can comfortably use both your hands.

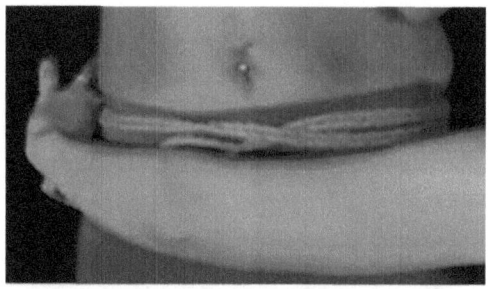

The next thing we want to do is make our leg loops so that we will go straight from there into the legs.

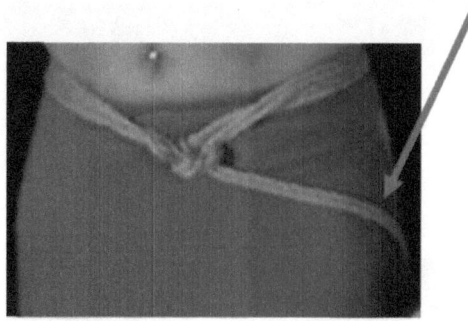

So again, ensure that the tying is form-fitting and avoid all square shapes. So follow the contour of the muscle and then go underneath the buttocks.

Put your finger in the indicated position to bring the rope up.

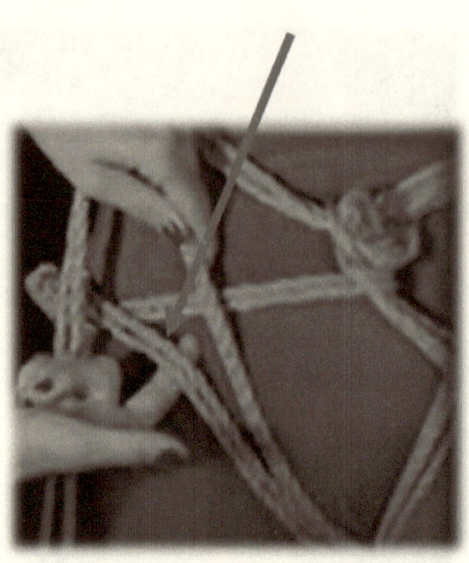

And grabbing onto that tension there and pulling the rope out completely.

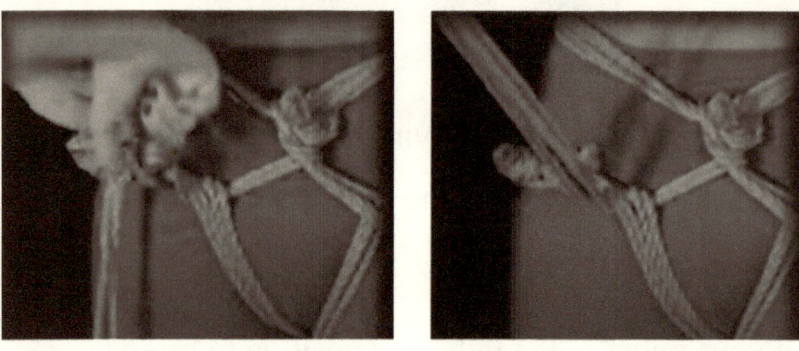

So you would do your single-column tie and then have to reinforce your bite for suspension.

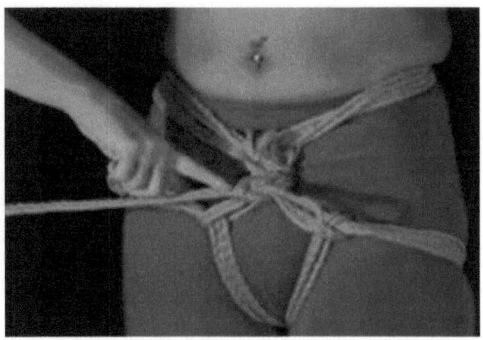

You would do that, or one way to do this straightforwardly is to feed a little bit of your working end through the bight.

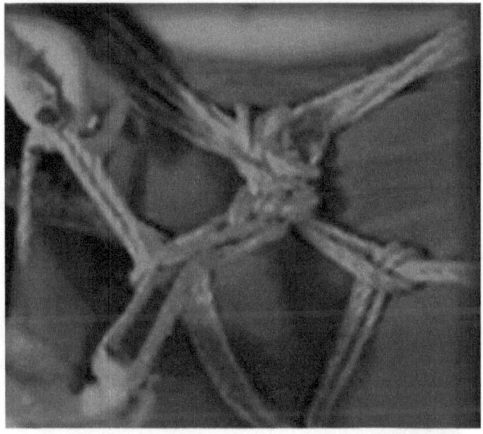

So when suspending off of a hip harness, you may like the suspension a little bit lower.

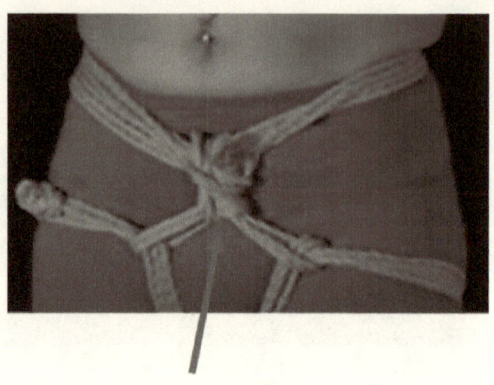

So it is not so straining on the back.

And you may want the knot by the side to sit on the butt dimple, so when you like to push your leg outwards, you get a crease.

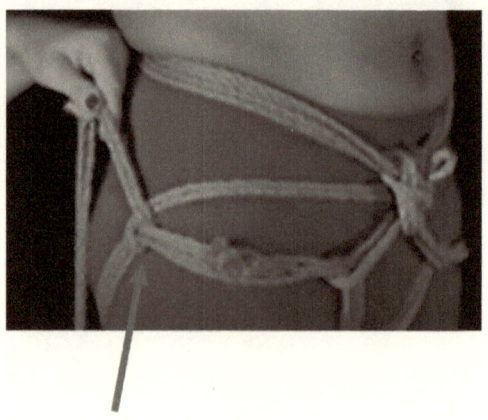

So that is where you want your knot to sit because it will be most comfortable.

Feel the tension to ensure it is nice and tight; everything looks nice, stiff, and solid at the front.

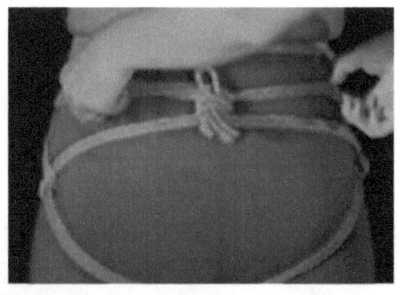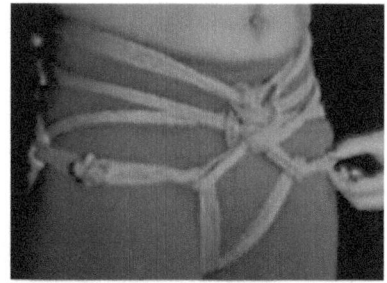

The third rope is there as a pattern to offer structure, so you can get a little bit adventurous and make up your third rope pattern in this harness; there is freedom for that.

Single column tie

We take the rope and find the middle to tie the single column. Almost every time begins from that.

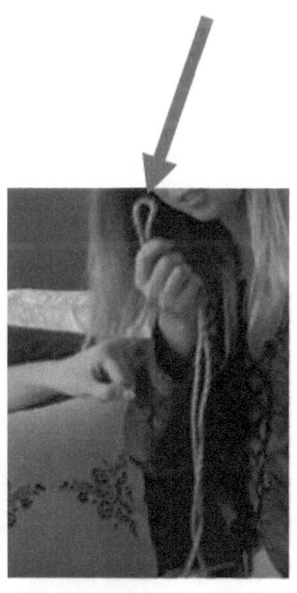

Then we wrap the rope around the wrist, not on the bones, a little higher, wrap it twice, and then you are holding your ropes here.

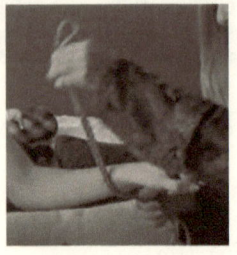 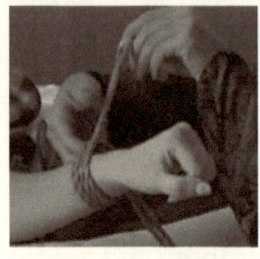 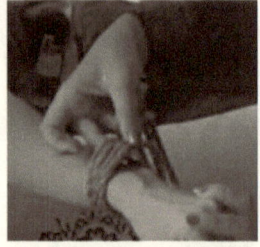

So holding it, then cross the bight, and this goes under everything like that, and then you tighten this knot.

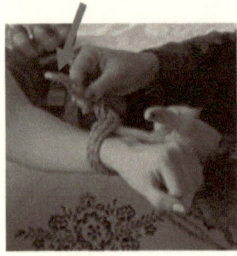 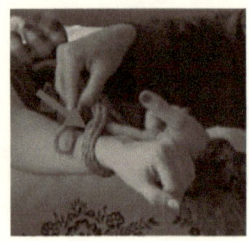 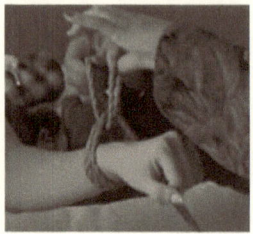

And that will produce a lovely shape. Always check your knot before continuing.

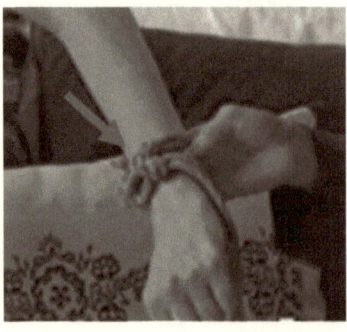

Also, you must check that your single-column tie is not twisted and that the knot does not tighten.

Make sure the rope is straight and not too tight. In between, a finger should be able to come through the ropes and the body.

Double column

The next important one is a double column, which is two hands. Take the middle of the rope and we wrap it around the wrists twice. We need to cross our ropes, and this bight goes all around all the ropes there.

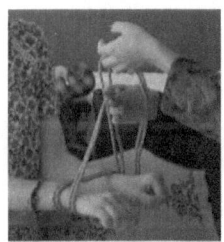 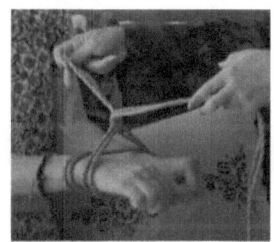 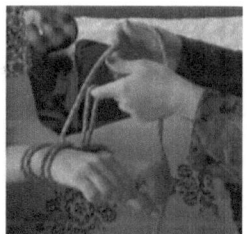

Then, tighten the knot. This pattern is the double column.

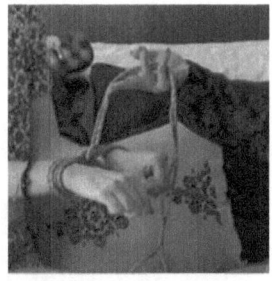

These few steps are the beginning; you can wrap the rope around your model using your imagination. However, before starting anything else in Shibari, you must know these basic knots.

For example, we can start from the wrist and put the hand over the chest to the shoulder.

Start tying by just wrapping the rope around the model. Feel the rope where it goes, and communicate with the model about how tight or loose it is to make it. Try to get close to your model; when you use the rope like that, you probably want to do it slowly. You can do it slowly or faster so our model feels how tight the rope can be, and then we make it a little looser but not loosen it up completely. Keep the tension very important because you do not want to lose it.

That is how you can use the rope to make it tighter or looser, get the feeling of you on your model's body, and show her that you are here closer.

We can try techniques such as applying some counter tension to your rope. Start by putting the hand on the body and pulling the rope up. Hold it, and then wrap the rope around the model.

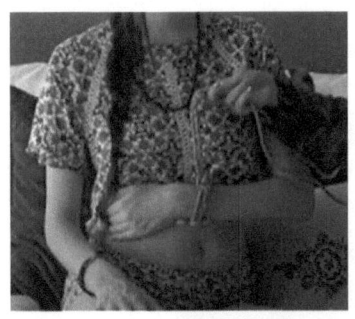 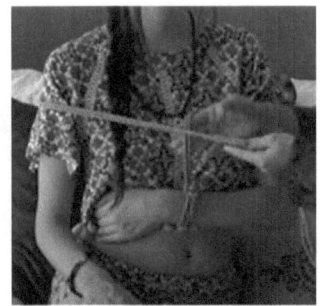

Then, apply the counter tension to pull the rope through and go in a different direction.

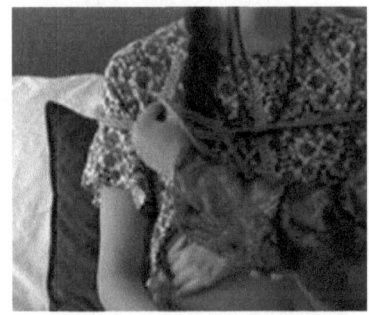

If the rope was going in a direction before, change it and bring it back to the other direction. Make sure the knot is in the middle. Also, remember the safety guide before doing this size because this body part is susceptible. And you can do more.

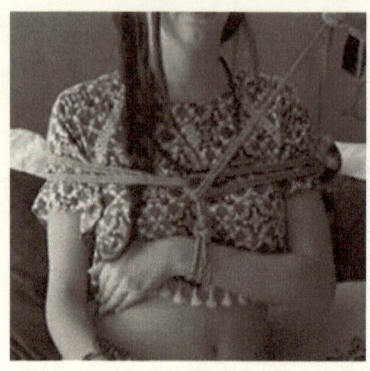

And quickly lock the rope. Tighten the knot up with the other rope end a couple of times to hold it.

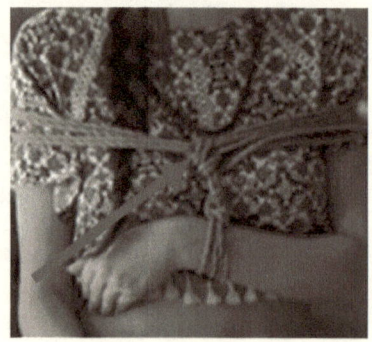

The main thing here is that when you tie a model, you need that effect of chilling because that is why you want to tie. You want to give your model a feeling of complete relaxation. So when you make the knot more complicated, tie it more, and try to support your model from some side so she can relax and not think about anything; that is the purpose. There are many techniques for letting the rope go in the opposite direction and a lot to explore.

Feel the mood

Another thing you need to know is that in Shibari, you can learn the knots and the complicated ties. But if you are not going with a flow, it will not affect your model because you are doing it for the moment.

The model leads you to what you need to do; you do it depending on her mood and character. For instance, what she is feeling today and even body language will show you a lot, and you are the one who is doing things for her. So, like being the rope, you are doing something for your model, not for yourself.

Flow tips

Your model should direct you, and you should not do just what you want. You do it because you want to make a person feel good; that is your number one thing to do: make your model feel good.

There are different ways to go with the flow if we are talking about the actual mood of a person. Let us take a couple of examples.

Your model was, for example, feeling sad or a little bit upset, and something was not going right. She needed company, a hug, or just being with herself a little more. Then, we will pull the body close to itself and be close to it while tying. We will probably start by tying the hands together but tie them in the front because we want the model to hug herself. Probably start from the hand and then go around tying it all together; maybe make a front prayer tie.

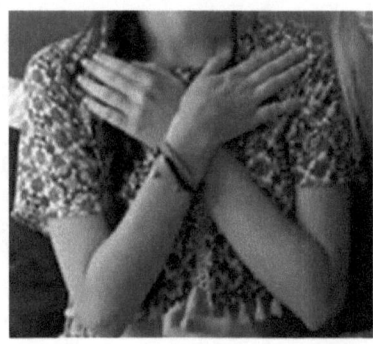

Being close to the model the whole time will make her feel relaxed and comfortable.

Another example is if she was feeling unconfident, this happens to girls. She looks at herself and does not like herself today. Shibari can also help with that. So, be very close again and tie the model to show your body the best. Maybe have a mirror somewhere there so she can see herself, look at it, and enjoy the view. And then she will relax and get it all back and get inspired.

On the ankle

So, we are trying to use a single column on the ankle.

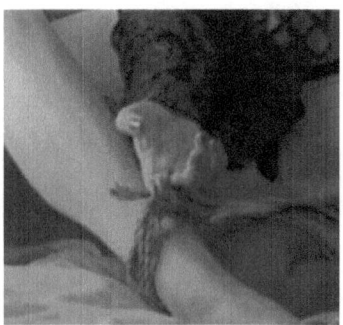

So this is a pretty loose single column, but it does not matter how loose it is. Bring the ankle in a lotus position just closer to you and wrap the rope around the waist.

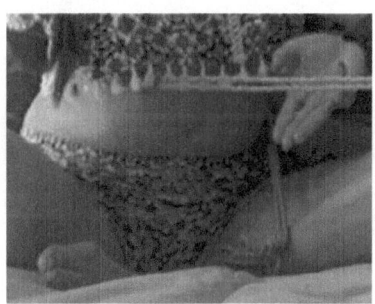

Next, apply counter tension.

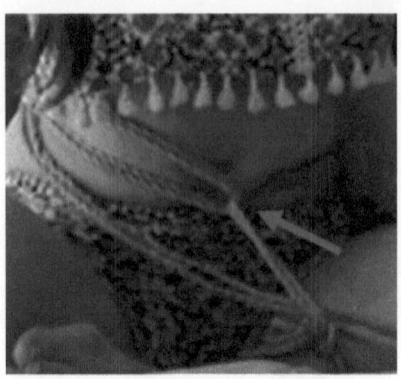

You should not make your rope lose. And then apply the counter dash again.

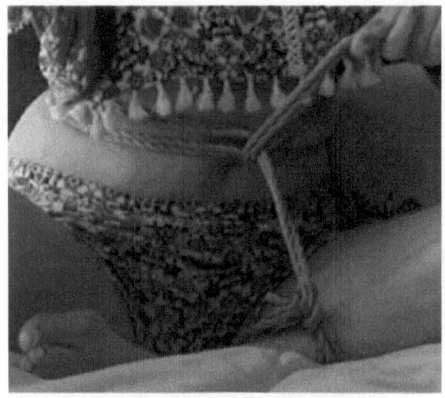

Fix the rope just by wrapping it around the rope. Also, when doing something close to the skin, have your fingers here to ensure your rope is not burning your model's body.

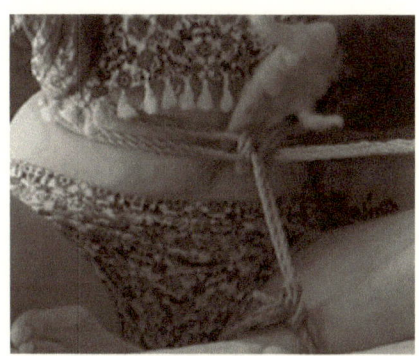

And here we will wrap that. We can wrap that around this rope to look like a handle.

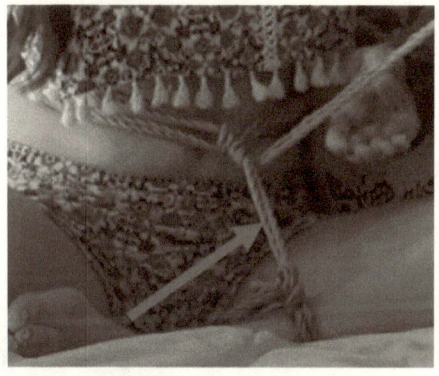

Or we can go on and wrap that around the leg.

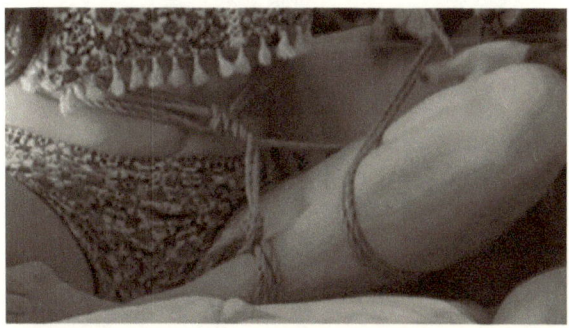

When you wrap, make sure that you keep the tension for just a couple of reps. When we untie, we do it slowly and carefully, giving this sensation of growth to the body because untying sometimes takes longer than tying. Also, you do not want to burn your model.

Tips on Knots and wraps

The direction of the wraps

so the first thing we start with is the direction things take once you've made the tie. You need to respect the rule of where the rope wants to go to make things work nicely and be aesthetically pleasing. The direction of the wrap, in other words, the bight on top or bottom, makes the difference.

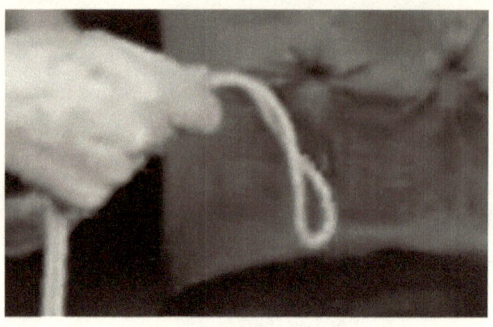

Grip the rope in a way to keep everything flat.

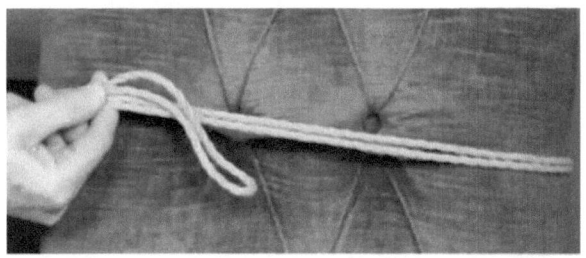

Push the rope around and change hands if necessary for convenience.

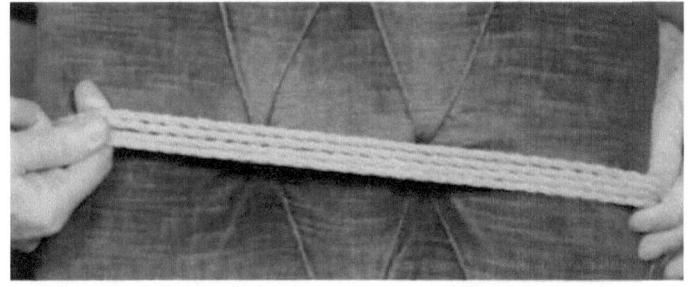

Slide the fingers around, keeping the wraps nice.

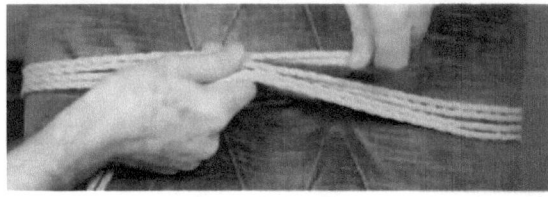

Keep it flat, working it around to get to the position dome to tie off.

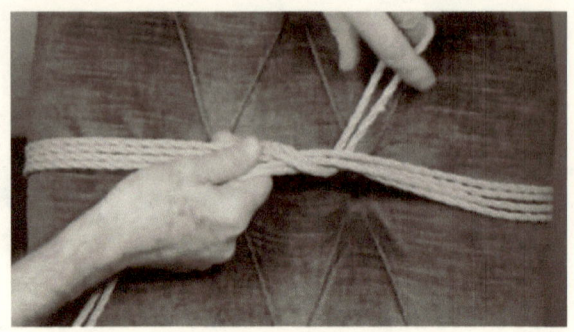

Firstly, make my loop on the right side, which will bring up the second point to form the correct knot—keeping the rope in the same hand and making my loop.

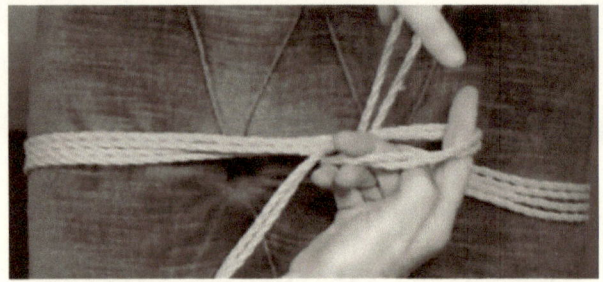

Then, take the rope through.

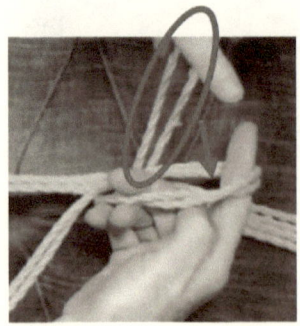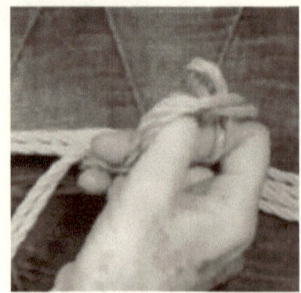

And tighten the knot.

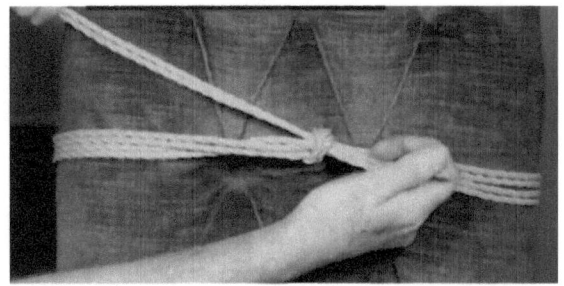

Flatten it all out, and from the directions, the rope wants to exit on the top.

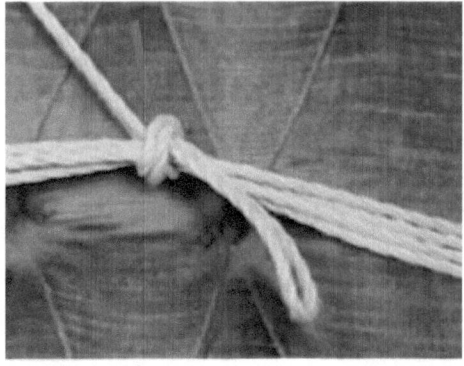

But if we want to work downwards, all the bindings start to twist.

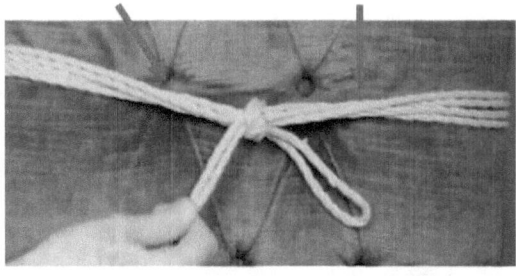

So your rope will exit on the side your bight is; in other words, it started at the top and worked downwards.

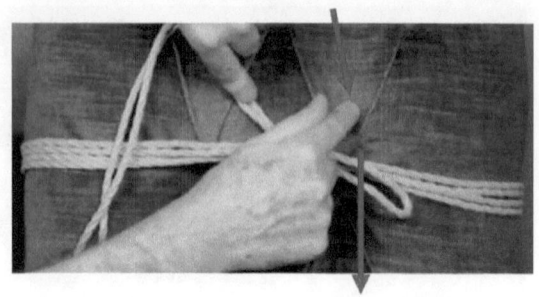

The bight stayed on the top; therefore, the rope exited from the top.

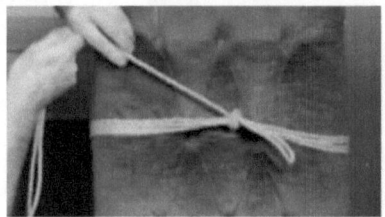 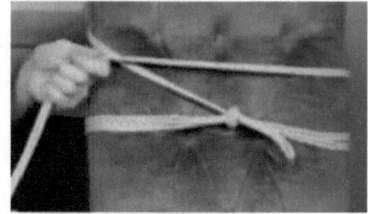

This pattern would work well if going to work upwards from here, create something else, and maybe bind that together.

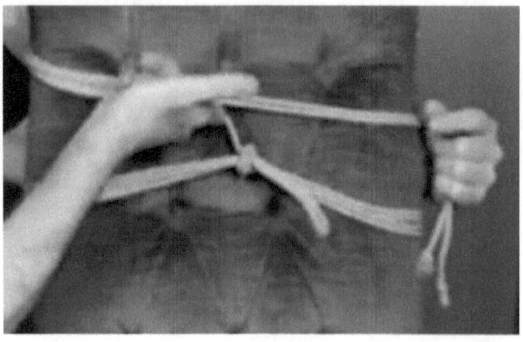

The image (below) shows that the rope wants to go in a specific direction (pointed out by the arrow).

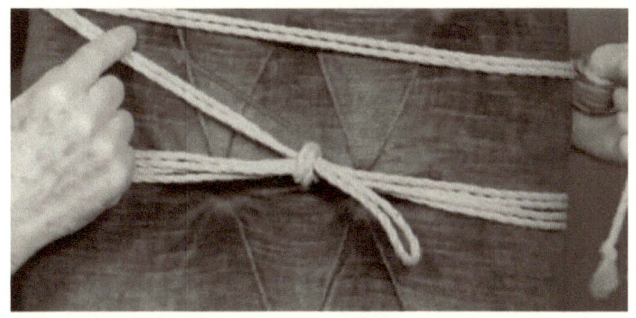

If we put the bight on the bottom, the rope will want to go downwards. To achieve that with the bight on the bottom, cross them.

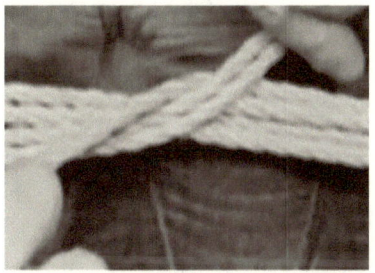 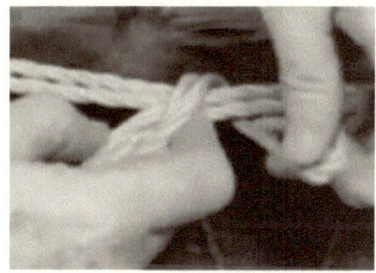

Again, use the same hand with the longer rope part, make a loop, and pull the bight through.

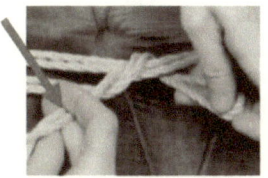 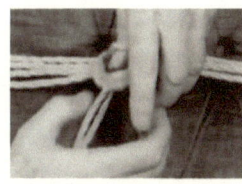 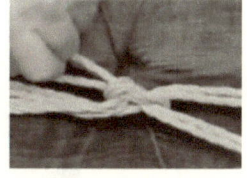

We want it to exit on the bottom without rolling the wraps over and making things look ugly.

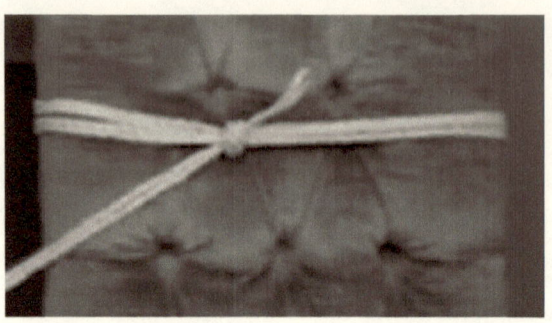

Getting the right knot

This part of getting the correct knot is an important point. Everybody always gets confused about how to form the most effective knot, the hon musubi or a granny knot in English. However, one that does not collapse so quickly and that is not a reef knot.

Let us show an excellent and simple rule for it. The rope wrap (image below) shows that our bight is on the top.

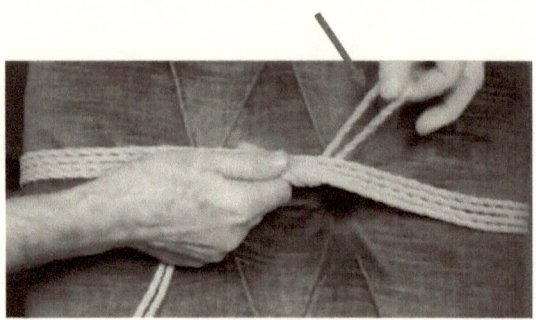

We must create a loop on the same side to form the most effective one. With a hand movement, make a loop with the long rope part, take the end, and close.

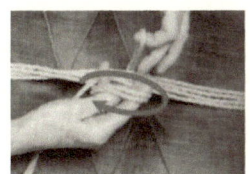 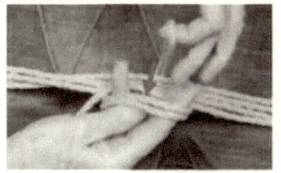 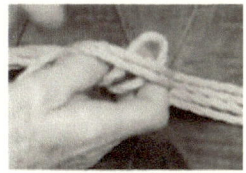

We got the correct version because the loop was on the right side, the same as the bight.

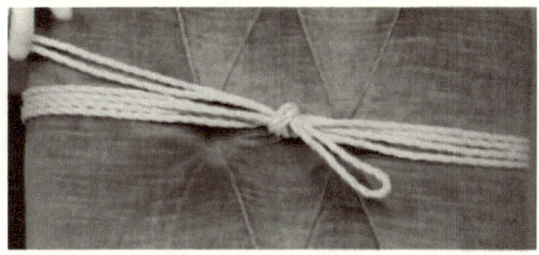

So that is the correct pattern, with both loop and bight on this side.

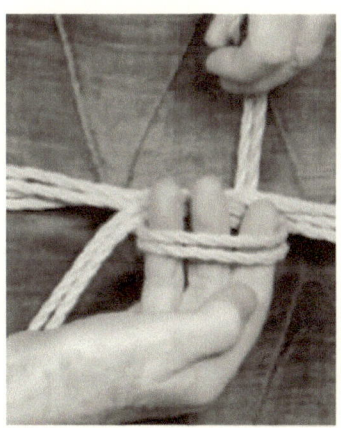

However, if we make the loop the other way and pull the bight through,

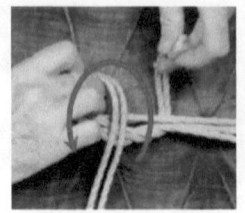 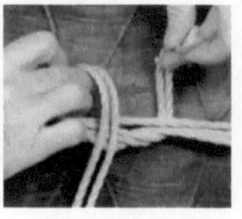 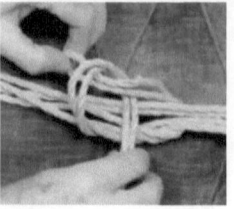

Settle up and arrange the rope, and flatten the necessary points.

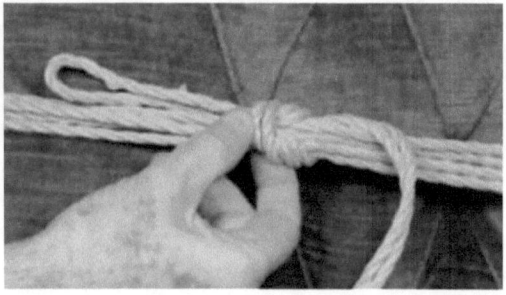

We can see the W shape of the brief knot, which, if pulled out, collapses.

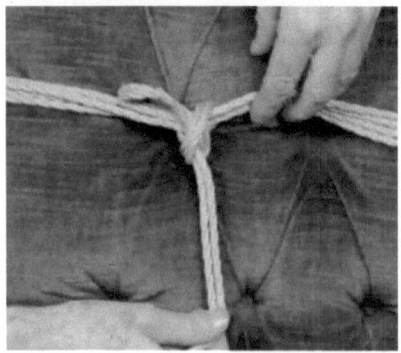

So, a simple rule: as long as you have both your loops on the same side, you will have the right knot.

Avoid changing hands

The third rule, which is expected almost always, is not to change hands any more than you need to. The more you switch hands, the less efficient you become. So try to develop a method that does not have to swap hands; you always have the rope in the right hand. So, for example, we are passing a rope around,

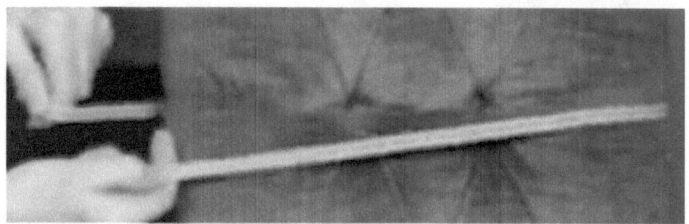

Change hands,

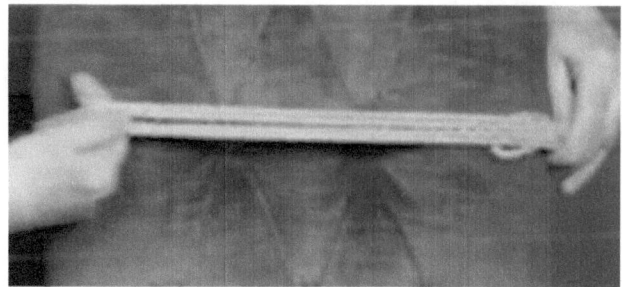

Slide back but maintain tension; cross the same hand here,

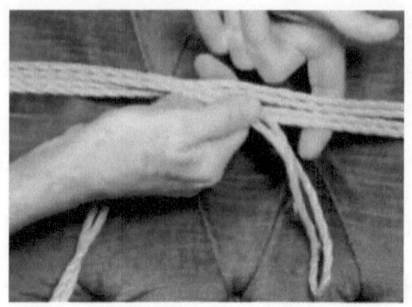

Form a loop and close.

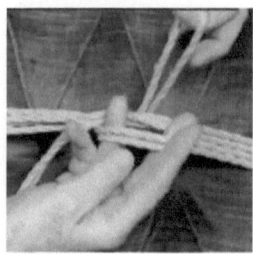 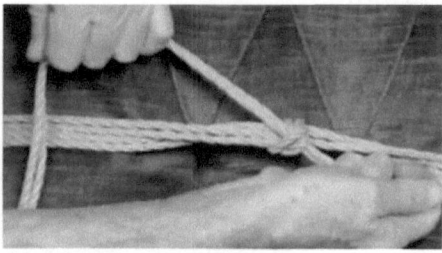

So that is the most efficient way to do that.

Tighten parallel to wrap

The fourth point is the direction you tighten the knot; always pull parallel to the wraps.

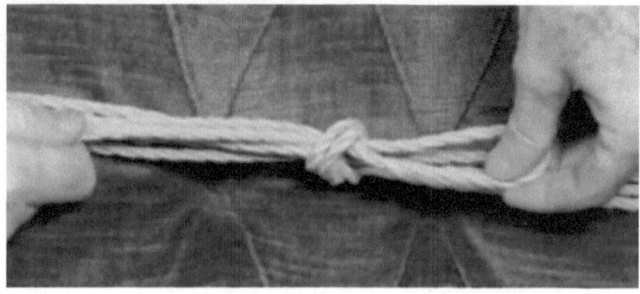

Remember, keep the bight stationary and pay attention to it. Then, you can tighten the knot a little further if you need to get a tight one. For example, when you tie the wrist, you will pull on each one, then the other.

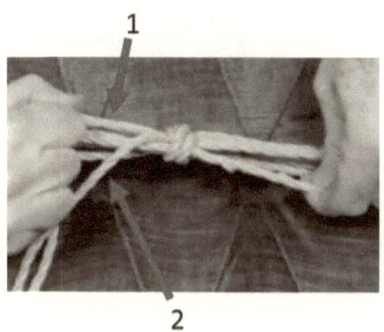

You may notice they moved a little, even after tightening them. This movement is because a common mistake people make is that they will reverse the direction, which is not very secure when pulled incorrectly.

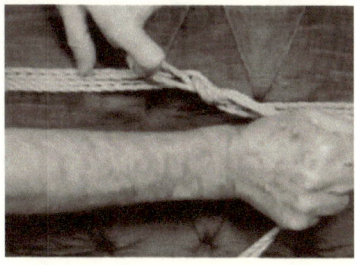

It can even collapse entirely and make all sorts of horrible messes if you do not respect the direction.

You can see the direction the rope wants to go; always remember to follow the way the rope wants to go. It is a tangible way, and you will always be correct.

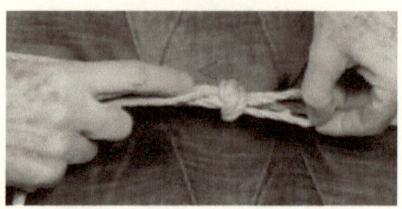

Do not roll your wraps

Be careful to try and keep equal tension on the bight and working end.

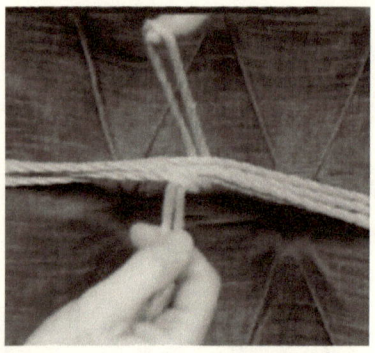

There is a tendency; if you pull too much on one, you roll everything over.

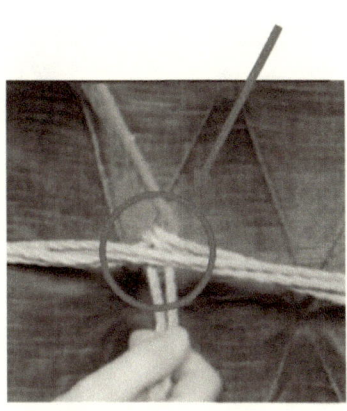

So be aware of keeping your tension distributed about the center.

Finger, do not fist

When you tie, minimize the number of fingers you use for efficiency. Try using two fingers or just one finger.

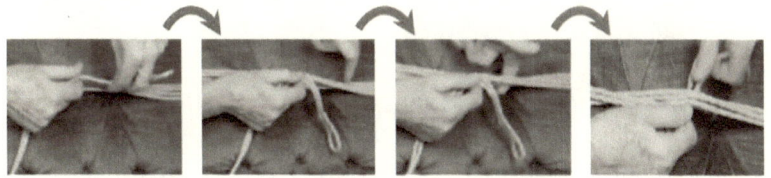

Again, when untying, try using one or two fingers; that is all it takes.

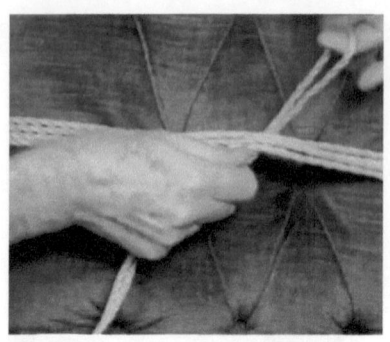

Pull, do not push

When you are making your tie, pull the rope. It is much more elegant than trying to push it up.

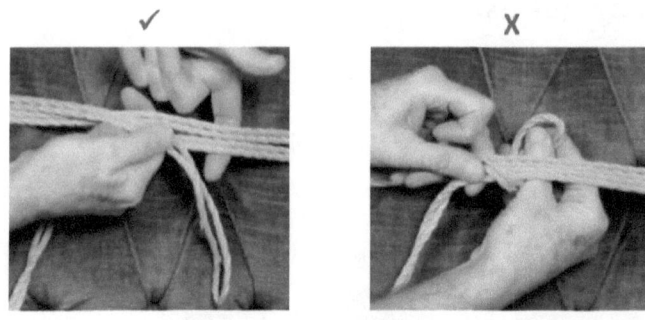

It is much easier to pull rope than it is to push it as well.

Changing direction

For example, the rope naturally wants to exit where the knot will.

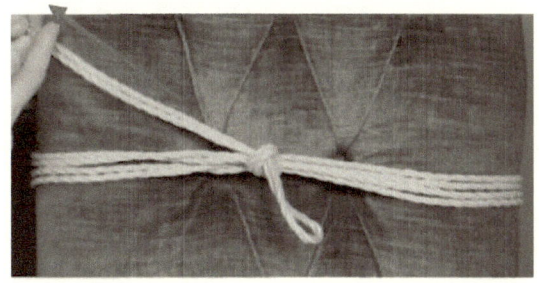

If we want to go the other way, it pulls the rope away in an ugly manner.

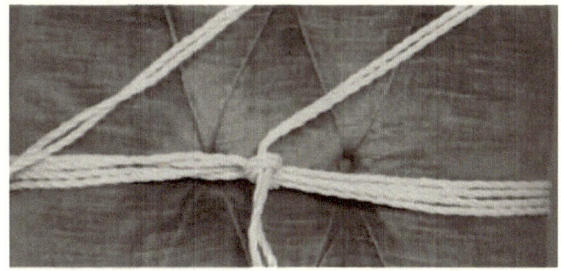

How do we change direction? The answer is to form an extra loop, and the way to know which way to do it is to put the rope in the route you want it to go and then take the bight through.

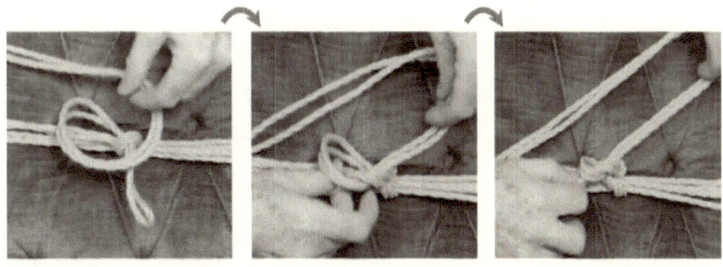

The rope goes off in the opposite direction if you want.

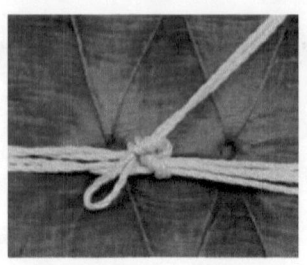

The correct way of going down is where you start. In other words, where the bight is with the wraps will determine how your rope exits. You can do a little bit of an ugly bulge bringing the rope down,

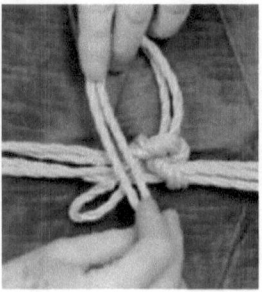

And then just close.

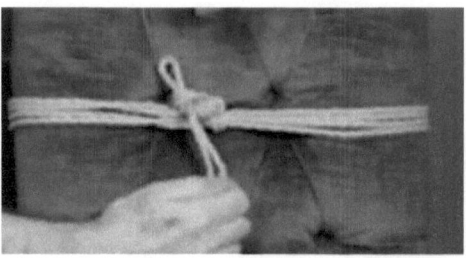

The problem is that it will roll the wraps over. So, it is better not to do it; you are better off starting in the correct direction.

Pay attention to these small details that make a big difference in how your rope looks at the end of the day.

Another way to wrap

The second method is probably better for tying on areas you travel above tension because you need to track the bight.

Wrap the rope and reach around. When you get to this point, you decide which direction you want to wrap in, which will determine which side to go.

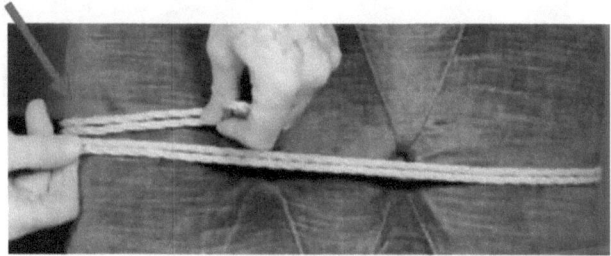

So, for example, if we want to go down, we must ensure to trap the bight underneath.

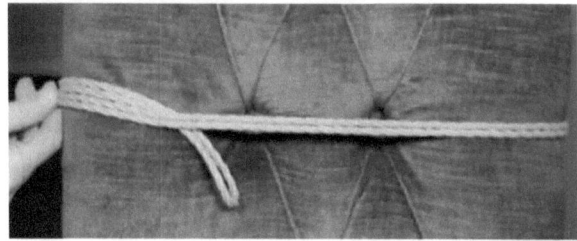

Come around with the rope again and pull the bight out afterward.

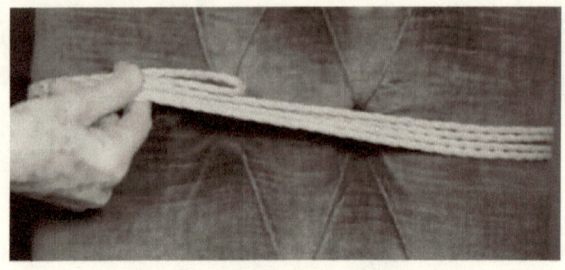

Slide it to where we want to go, make the loop, and close it off.

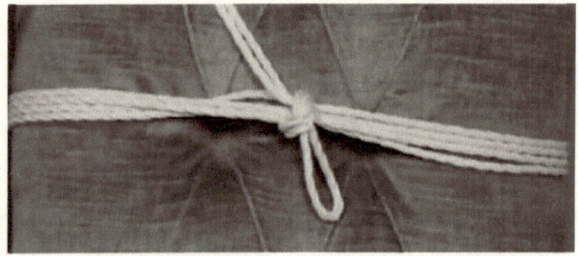

If we start with the bight underneath, we get the opposite result, the rotor going in the opposite direction. So to achieve that, work up to trap the bight this way.

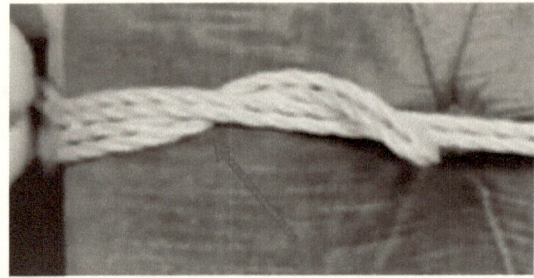

And then work upwards. Trap everything and move it across the cross and tie first.

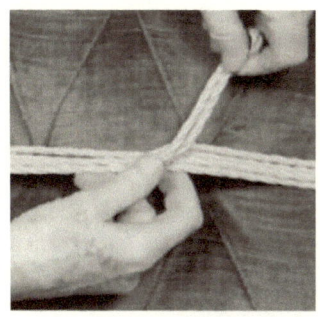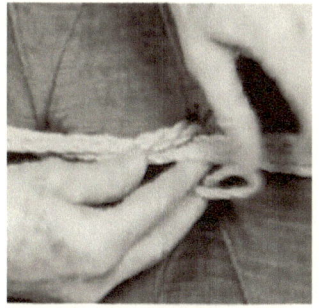

This time, notice that the rope is coming down.

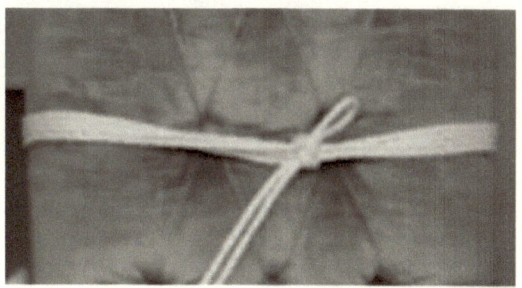

For the two ways, play around with them and see what you like best; neither is right nor wrong. However, you cannot track the bight if you are tying wrists and there is too much room for the slide round; better methods exist.

Quick "kiddy's gun" method

This technique is a quick method for tying this tie. It depends on your working direction, so try it out and see how it works. We tend to use it for applying hands behind the back for a boxed tie. Pair the rope up from underneath at the back of the arms and work from right to left. This method is fast when tying a box tie, where the arms are parallel behind, and you are tired of winding around the wrists. So start from underneath.

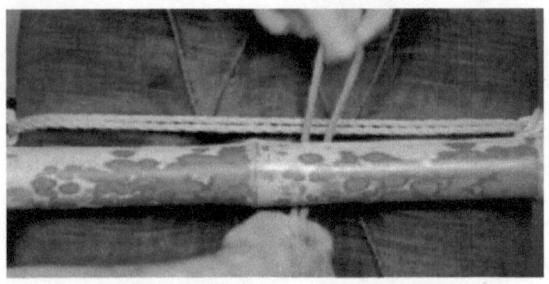

Catch the rope, and do that again, allowing some safety space.

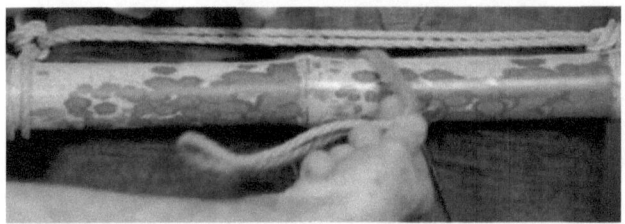

Pass the rope up to the fingers and make your adjustments.

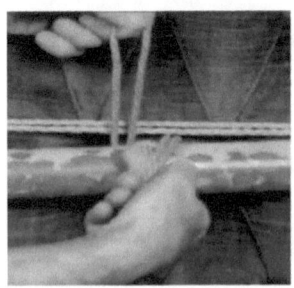
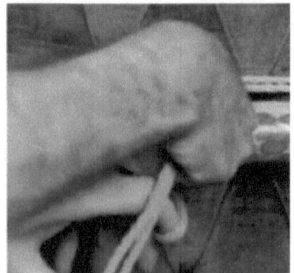

Using a finger, pass through the gap, catch it, and take it underneath.

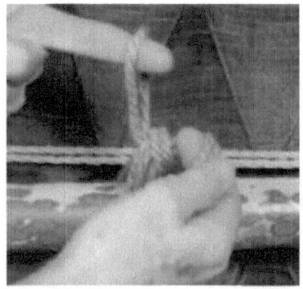

And now to make Kitty's gun, careful not to roll this not over.

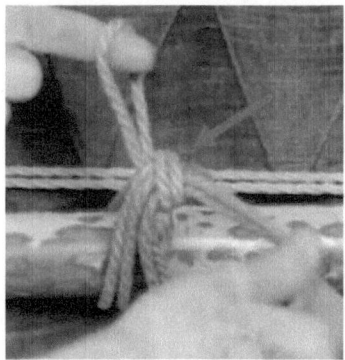

Over the thumb, make the gap slightly more significant to make life easier, and then flick the bight through.

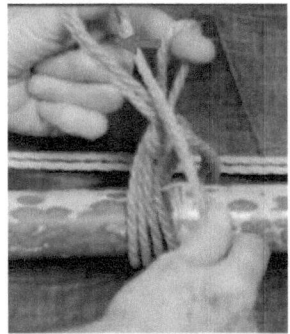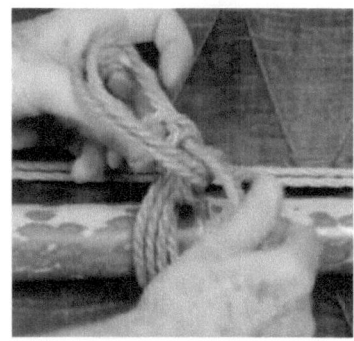

Then, holding the bight in position to add some tension,

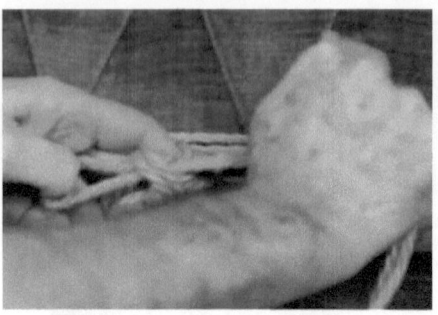

And there we have it.

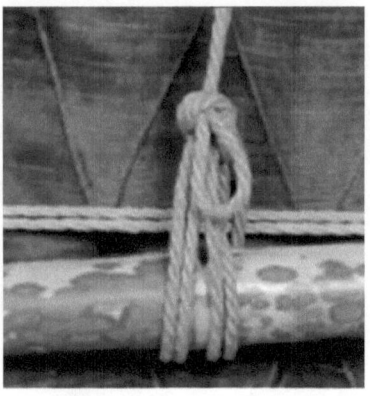

Chapter Nine

Exploring other Aesthetic Ties

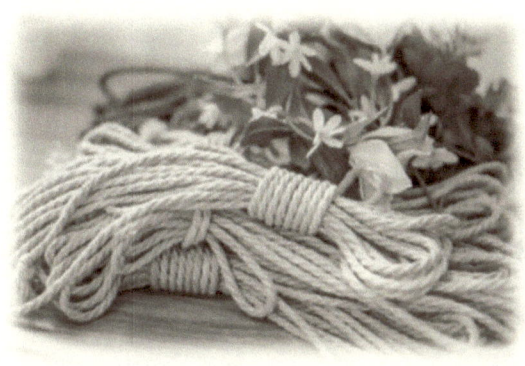

The introduction to decorative ties involves several layers of exploration:

＋ Defining Decorative Ties

The artistic manipulation of cords, ropes, and knots for decorative reasons is called decorative tying. In this enthralling art form, the creator uses their hands as creative tools to painstakingly create elaborate patterns that inspire feelings, narratives, and meaning. These ties are more than just arrangements; they combine technique and creativity to create visually breathtaking compositions that represent the artist's vision and the beauty of the human form. Inviting onlookers to explore the harmony between art and the human canvas as the ropes gracefully envelop the body, they celebrate the union of technical prowess and artistic spirit.

✦ Historical Context

Aesthetics are innately human, transcending cultures and civilizations, as shown through the history of art. Artistic expressions have connected us across time and geography through the millennia by reflecting profoundly on our shared human experience.

✦ Cultural Significance

Several nations have used decorative ties to convey cultural identities, beliefs, and rituals. These elaborate works of art served as body ornaments and symbolic representations of the nations they represented.

✦ Fusion of Art and Function

The seamless fusion of artistic inventiveness and practical functionality is best shown in decorative ties, which turn everyday objects into eye-catching examples of human ingenuity.

✛ Artistic Evolution

Decorative ties have changed from merely functional to elaborate works of art, expressing the rich tapestry of human ingenuity and culture over the decades. A dynamic interaction between artistic innovation and cultural influences has fueled this progress. Decorative ties have evolved from serving practical functions in daily living to manifestations of individuality and societal values. These complex storylines are now braided through tradition and modern imagination threads. As methods changed and improved, ornamental ties were used to embellish useful items and the essence of cultural heritage, conveying memories and feelings over time.

✛ Art's Universal Nature

Artistic inventiveness is a basic aspect of human culture that has persisted throughout civilizations.

✛ Early Examples and Cultural Diversity

The merging of creative styles is seen in historical art periods like the Early Middle Ages. The practice of decorative ties mirrors the diverse range of cultures and their artistic expressions.

♣ Event Management

The idea of cultural events illustrates the value of art and aesthetics in many communities.

One can appreciate decorative ties' inherent significance as creative expressions that cross time and cultural barriers by comprehending their historical, cultural, and artistic dimensions.

Basic Chest Harness

Creating a Basic Chest Harness involves a harmonious blend of artistic considerations and technical techniques:

♣ Design Elements

It is essential to comprehend design principles like balance, symmetry, and proportion when creating a harness that looks good.

♣ Visual Arts and Aesthetics

The harness appears better overall when visual arts principles like color harmony and balance are applied.

✛ Aesthetic Principles

Aesthetic factors, including material textures and color selections, influence the aesthetic impact of the harness.

✛ Technical Proficiency

Technical knowledge and creative creativity are essential to create a practical and artistic harness.

✛ Materials and Techniques

The harness's structural integrity is influenced by the materials chosen, such as ropes and knots, and the techniques used.

✛ Historical Inspiration, Fashion and Art Applications

The sculpture gains depth and cultural complexity by drawing inspiration from old chest harness designs. Basic Chest Harnesses are used in performances, installations of art, and even fashion, giving these fields a distinctive touch. A Basic Chest Harness can be both a useful accessory and an artistic statement that connects to fashion and art by fusing design principles, aesthetics, and technical mastery.

Styles and Techniques

Numerous tying techniques have emerged due to various cultures and rituals, each with distinct symbolic meaning and visual appeal. For instance, the delicate designs used in Japanese Shibari express sensuality and beauty. Indian Pitha, on the other hand, uses intricate limb-tying techniques to represent ceremonies and devotion. These fashions act as aesthetic and cultural expressions, showcasing the variety of human inventiveness.

❖ Aesthetics Integration

It takes a certain artistic skill to include beauty in limb tying. Enhancing the overall artistic quality greatly benefits from using colors, patterns, and textures. While elaborate patterns can reflect cultural symbols or narrate stories, vivid colors inspire specific emotions. Textures improve tactile experiences and provide visual appeal and more depth. Practitioners turn limb tying into a complex visual tale by carefully choosing and combining various components.

❖ Safety Measures

Safety must always come first when using limb-tying techniques. To avoid danger or discomfort, proper practices are crucial. It is essential to understand human anatomy, pressure points, and circulation. It is crucial to use the right materials that will not hurt. Learning from seasoned professionals or subject-matter experts offers crucial direction to minimize risks and improve the overall experience.

❖ Cross-Cultural Influences

Limb tying acts as a blank canvas for global stimuli. It displays the complex tangle of various customs, aesthetics, and practices. A diverse fusion of styles and meanings is produced due to the contributions made by various cultures and geographical areas. The art form is further enriched through cultural interchange, resulting in hybrid practices that cut over geographical boundaries.

❖ Cultural Significance

Beyond its physicality, binding limbs have great cultural and ceremonial significance. It is used in ceremonies, performances, and symbolic representations throughout many civilizations. Limb tying develops into a visual language for expressing cultural myths, tenets, and histories. It is a form of expression that captures the spirit of custom and heritage.

❖ Fashion and Art

Limb tying's crossover into fashion and art results from its integration of art and purpose. It functions as a distinctive statement piece in fashion, bringing mystery and originality to ensembles. It challenges norms and pushes boundaries in art by obfuscating the distinction between form and function. Fashion and artistic expression gained a new level thanks to the beauty and meaning of limb tying.

❖ Cultural Exchange

Tying styles and aesthetics converge and change as cultures encounter them. New hybrid practices are created due to cultural exchange, each reflecting the interaction of many influences. This contact encourages mutual understanding and appreciation of cultural variety and broadens the aesthetic palette.

We obtain profound insights into the rich and multifaceted art of limbs through the analysis of many styles, the integration of aesthetics, the focus on safety, and the comprehension of cross-cultural influences. This technique goes beyond purely physical expression to incorporate cultural, artistic, and symbolic representations, urging us to recognize the deep relationships between tradition and human creation.

❖ Aesthetics vs. Functionality

Understanding the complex interaction between aesthetic value and usefulness in decorative rope techniques is key to exploring aesthetic ties. This harmony, shown in the contrast between aesthetics and practicality, combines artistic expression and practical intent. We can see how form and function come together by examining case studies from diverse fields, such as Islamic architecture, art therapy, and architecture. These studies highlight the need for designs to be aesthetically pleasing and practical to accomplish their intended goals. Islamic decorations are an example of how aesthetic value and spiritual and theological importance can coexist.

❖ Evolving Trends

An interesting trip into the tremendous influence of modern artists, technology, and multidisciplinary collaborations on the artistic landscape can be had by investigating the changing trends in decorative rope techniques. Artists nowadays are defying the limitations of traditional approaches and starting a revolutionary journey. A symbiotic link between innovation and tradition characterizes this creative renaissance, as artists deftly incorporate new mediums and cutting-edge tools to create enthralling and visually arresting works of art. Interdisciplinary collaborations between architecture and technology have largely driven this evolution. Due to this convergence, integrating complex rope techniques into large-scale installations has given these techniques a renewed significance in bigger sizes.

In addition, technology has become a key enabler, opening up a new era of opportunities for ornamental rope creation. Innovations like 3D printing and computer design tools have opened up unexplored territories, enabling artists to experiment with complex rope combinations and previously inconceivable structural designs. The growing function of these techniques in modern art and design is highlighted, and this shift reverberates across exhibition halls and in museum announcements.

Helping people appear attractive and aesthetic

Photography and Rope bondage can change a person from being themselves daily to becoming a work of art. Particularly those who like the expression of art. If you develop a skill like knotting or tying, you can use it in various areas. For example, a rope can stop an unusual means if it comes in contact with no human models. Instead, using rope to hold objects helps to be more creative as one can suggest peculiar shapes.

＋ Demonstrable act

Another reason you should tie Shibari is that it allows one of the partners to dominate. Apart from the dominant individual possessing an affordable set of ropes and toys, they can use a demonstrable skill that requires patience and learning time. Showing patience, confidence, and skill with the rope will help you get started. It is also an excellent way to create friendships and obtain respect in the BDSM group.

✛ Versatility

For people who love to explore bondage, a rope is one of the versatile tools you can use. Toys for the bondage act are costly, instead of spending lots of dollars on expensive tools that can be used for restraining. They can use a rope to create gags, blindfolds, floggers, and any creative object. Then, when they finish the act, they can unwind it and use it for another thing before keeping their rope properly in a drawer.

Psychological and Societal Implications

Investigating the many facets of colorful rope techniques reveals a tapestry of social and psychological repercussions. A platform for various interpretations is provided by how semiotics and symbols interact to express deeper meanings, frequently influenced by cultural sensitivity. The visual and tactile qualities of rope arts can elicit feelings and relationships, having an intrinsic psychological impact on people.

Exploring Ethical Dimensions

As we go on to ethical considerations, a complicated network of permission, disputes, and ethical frameworks enter the picture. The agreement of the producers, users, and spectators becomes crucial, especially in works that may offend some people. Controversies from various viewpoints highlight the complex connection between art and society, reflecting shifting norms. Ethical frameworks guide discussions of appropriation, cultural sensitivity, and responsible creativity.

Future Directions

Looking ahead, the trajectory of ornamental rope techniques is characterized by new fashion trends, cutting-edge educational programs, and environmentally friendly practices. This creative form is poised to change due to collaborative projects, multidisciplinary learning, and increased environmental consciousness. As a result, the importance of aesthetic linkages goes beyond purely aesthetic considerations and resonates with psychology, culture, ethics, and future perspectives. Promising directions for further study are revealed when scholars travel among

183

various spheres, illuminating the continuing conversation between art, society, and human experience.

Chapter Ten

Unleashing Creativity with Freestyle and Advanced Shibari

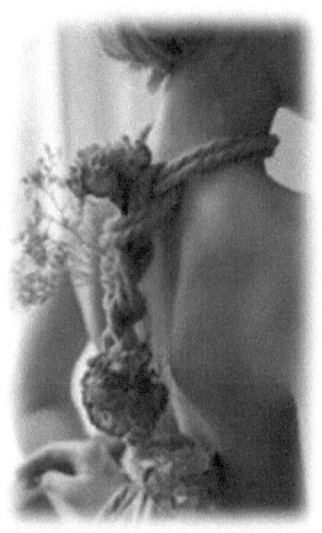

Building on Foundations, Creating Creative Expressions

In the universe of Shibari, developing fundamental skills is the first step toward artistic mastery; this crucial idea is emphasized in this part. Like a strong building requires a solid foundation, these fundamentals are a launching pad for imaginative inquiry and creativity. Knowledge of fundamental knots and ties goes beyond technical execution and equips practitioners to explore their creative side. Shibari artists use these basics to convey distinctive storylines through rope, just like a painter utilizes color theory.

Introducing partial suspensions, "Rising Above"

Shibari practices partial suspensions, which include elevating specific body parts with ropes while maintaining points of contact with the ground. Practically speaking, they facilitate a variety of body stances and leverage, increasing visual complexity. In a symbolic sense, "Rising Above" represents going above and beyond the call of duty, consistent with Shibari's creative spirit. This demonstrates how aesthetics and emotion coexist while using ropes to express stories. Partial suspensions help practitioners develop skills and strengthen the connection between technique, emotion, and inventiveness.

⬇ Embracing Asymmetry and Accessorizing: Playing with Imbalance

Shibari introduces a break from conventional balance by embracing asymmetry and combining accessories, opening new channels for artistic expression. By deviating from conventions, purposeful asymmetry gives designs vitality and challenges perceptions. This strategy increases intricacy and makes it possible to manipulate tension, focus points, and negative space. The ensuing interaction stirs feelings and fits with Shibari's use of ropes and the human form to communicate.

⊥ Expanding Creativity Through Weaving New Patterns

When it comes to Shibari, the pursuit of artistic development entails venturing into unexplored territory by deftly weaving fresh patterns and motifs. This topic highlights the transformative potential of going beyond conventional methods. It enables practitioners to open a world of innovative possibilities by enticing them to enter the world of experimenting.

The process of creating new patterns goes beyond technical proficiency. It becomes a doorway to unrestrained creativity, where creators can integrate their original viewpoints and feelings into their works. The ability to create complex narratives with ropes is discovered by practitioners who venture outside accepted standards and into uncharted territory.

This investigation includes the emotional and symbolic spheres and the physical ones. As new patterns develop, they can reflect individual experiences, arouse strong feelings, or tell intricate tales. This dynamic interaction between skill and emotion exemplifies Shibari's ability to speak on various levels.

This topic's importance comes from its call to embrace innovation and break down barriers. Practitioners embark on a voyage of self-discovery by creating novel patterns and designs that bring to life previously unimagined combinations that perfectly express their creativity. Shibari continues to develop creatively, reaffirming its status as a genre that develops alongside the artists who create it.

Processing and care of the rope

You will need a carabiner and a rope that you have tied on a post. You must use gloves if working with processing at least 10 to 12 ropes.

- ❖ Take one end of the rope. Take the carabinier and run the rope through the carabiner.
- ❖ With the end of the rope that is about 6 inches, twist it over the remaining part of the rope three times.
- ❖ Pull the short end of the rope and go see-saw back and forth. Do that about four times.

❖ Let go of the short end of the rope and hold it near the twist. See-saw back and forth again.

This process is going to break the fiber and soften the rope. After you have broken the ropes, the little hairs on it will break apart.

❖ Grab the rope from the bight. Hold it in a way that as you burn the rope, the flames can get between the ropes. Do this in a well-ventilated area. You can also get air filters or masks that you can put on because this process will create smoke.
❖ Turn on your gas or stove at a medium flame.
❖ Run the rope over the fire back and forth at four or five inches. Be careful not to burn the rope.
❖ Take the next four or five inches and do the same procedure.

After searing the rope, cleaning off the accumulated assets from burning is necessary. It is done by oiling the rope.

There are two ways to oil the rope;

1. Deep conditioning of the rope:

- Use a balm mixture of jojoba oil or mineral oil and wax.
- Please take a small quantity of it and apply it at the center of your palm.
- Run the rope through your palm.
- Keep applying, rubbing, and running it through your palm.
- Massage into the rope.

2. The external oiling with some olive oil:
- Pour a small amount of the oil into a rag and rub the oil through the rope. It keeps your rope toned and lubricated.

After oiling the rope, you have excess wax on the rope, and you cannot seem to get it off with the rag;

- Turn on your stove to 220. Bake the ropes for about 10 minutes.
- It will allow the oil and lubricant to absorb into the rope threads.
- Take the whole rope.
- Lay it in a pan with aluminum to prevent contact with the pan and burning.

Tips for riggers.

When dealing with ropes, the entire experience as a bottom or the top can be overwhelming because there is so much new information and concepts. So, getting a clear focus as a new rigger is good.

ⵜ No ego.

Understand that it is okay to set your ego aside sometimes. Set it aside, swallow it, learn, and grow. Sometimes, you may need to stand up for yourself or your bottom. That is a healthy, balanced ego. Have this rather than a negative toxic who will not allow you to learn and grow. If anybody tries to correct you, you should not get offended. Remember that along your journey, stay humble. Ropes take time to grow and learn things. It does take some financial investment. Remember that the pictures of the people you are looking at have gone through much practice and have put a lot of hours into it. You do not know the backgrounds, so do not hold yourself to those standards and do not think you will get there right from the beginning. You must work like any other skill, hobby, or anything you want to get good at. You also may not be the best. It is not a competition. Focus on your rope goals and create the experience you are trying to create. You are going to be a better rigger overall. While growing, you will die outside your skill level to try new things. However, ensure it is both your and your bottom's risk level. They should understand the risk of what can happen if it goes wrong. Ensure you have spotters around to be sure you are doing things safely.

+ Education.

You have to go to education to grow as a rigger. Not only do you need to understand the risks and the proper safety for doing things correctly and safely, but you also need to invest time and money into conventions of education within your community. Many cities have local educational rope groups that meet once, twice, or thrice a month. Some have rope socials where you can go and play like a rope play party. That is an excellent place to watch other people, learn, and see where the people in your community are. If you are struggling to find something, ask the people that you buy your rope. You can go to FetLife or ask for the people around you because some events are happening that are not on FetLife. FetLife may probably be 60% of what is happening in your community near you. FetLife only searches for events around the area in which your profile is located. If your profile location is probably Dallas, it will only look for things in a certain-mile radius around Dallas. If you live in a small town outside of that and search, you may not see any events in your area. It means you must change your profile from where you live to the most significant local city. You will probably find more events. There is a ton of rope education online. A rope is not just about learning patterns. There are theories and philosophies behind the rope. It is an overarching art; the best way to learn it is in a 'master to student' situation. It may not be accessible to the majority of people within the community. We have more kinds of mass-produced education, events, and conventions. Just remember that rope is not just about learning all of the patterns. It is also about understanding how and why they work. Understand in the future of your journey that, to get to the next level in rope, you will have to invest some money in intensive, private, and one-on-one education with experienced rope tops.

＋ Practice.

Find the things you want to focus on and practice them until you know them well. Practice to the point that you can simultaneously tie with the same tension and all of your wraps. For example, practice a single column that includes your hip, chest, and whatever you do. Try it and perfect it before moving on to different styles and techniques. Find the one that works and perfect it. Practice while you are watching video practices. Practice on any surface, on the chair, or on a pillow. Buy a dummy if you do not have a partner. You would grow faster. You can attend the same educational class as someone in a year, and if you practice four times a week and they are practicing two times a week, you will probably know and understand things better.

Learning ropes does take time, practicing over and over again. Tying rope, trying rope, and discussing rope get you better daily. If you want to practice something new, like a suspension, do it at an event with more experienced riggers. Ask them, "I am going to try this new thing. Do you mind observing or being there in case of an emergency?" You can also ask them to give you feedback on what you could have done better. Some people may not want to practice new things in front of an audience at an event. However, that is the safest place to do it. You may want to do it at home and perfect it, but something might go wrong, and you would not know what to do.

+ Listen.

Listen not only to the voices in your head like 'You should do this, or you should not do that, but it is also risky,' but listen to your bottoms as they communicate to you. Listen to how more experienced people are doing it. Listen to more experienced rope tops when they give you advice. Try not to let your ego or feelings get in the way of you still being able to take and learn something positive from the experts. They may probably correct you not in the most polite way to correct your rope or try to give you some advice. Take the advice still. Take the knowledge because that is the goal that you are aiming towards. Listen when other people are talking casually about rope theory or concepts. You could pay attention and then go to rope events where rope people talk about these things.

+ Take care of your bottoms.

Take care of them emotionally, mentally, physically, and psychologically. They are your 'life partner.' Please ensure they get particular care, the aftercare and the beforecare. They also need particular 'during' care. They need a small quantity of time outside of just trying to communicate. You are going to learn more from your bottoms than anything else. Handling a rope is not easy, and it is stressful. However, you must take care of your bottoms and be aware of what is happening to them because it might be physically strenuous. So, if you want to be a good rigger from the beginning, know the importance of taking care of your bottom.

Shibari in water guide
1. As soon as your rope gets wet, it gets tighter. If you have a harness on a model, the model going to the pool or taking a shower will make the rope tighter. Putting tied-up models in water is more dangerous than ropes

in general. You need safety scissors at all times, especially when ropes are wet. Although a little mistake can happen, and the rope affects the breathing nerve, you are prepared because you have scissors.

2. When water impacts the fiber rope, it weakens and damages the ropes. You need to note that rope that gets wet should never be used for suspension in the future. This is because the fibers expand and loosen from their original.

3. If you use colored ropes, the rope can lose color. It would start with literally dripping that color from itself. It can get awkward if you are in a public pool and your ropes are red, blue, green, or brown. Be aware of the fact that ropes can leak with their color. It does not happen to natural rope like jute. However, if it has color, it is most likely to drip. It depends on the producer of the rope. There is no way to prevent this than to use a natural rope. If you are doing a photo shoot, do a photo shoot when you are in the water, not when you get out. It is because it is going to be dripping all over. When you untie that, your hands will be the color of your rope. The color from your hand

197

could last for like 2 or 3 days. You can also use the Passion Craft store rope in water; that rope will not leak and won't lose color.

4. When your rope is wet, it will be challenging to untie. It is because the ropes get tighter. Making it easier for yourself is not to tie actual knots. You could tie flat knots or maybe do twirls or twists. It would be very much easier to take off your model. You can untie your ropes in the water or shower.

5. Another thing to note is that even if you put your ropes in water and think that water will clean them just like that, you will still need to wash them afterward. It will drop almost everywhere, especially if you have colored rope. If you do not dry it properly, it will still stain other clothes. After doing ropes in water, put your rope in the water again, but wash it. You also need to wash it, mainly if you use salty water. Wash your rope and dry it properly.

6. Do not dry your rope in the open sun. It is not too suitable for your rope. Do not also be afraid of using your ropes in water.

Pronounced satisfaction

There are so many degrees of satisfaction in using a rope. You have the chance to master your rope, learn the intricacies, the way it moves, and the method of controlling it, and you have the opportunity to use your knowledge and mastery to influence and affect other people. Practical domination of the rope and the individual you intend to control.

Provide opportunities for relationships.

Knowing how to use rope bondage can pave the way for doorways and usher you into relationships you may not have. Since not many people around can tie the rope, people with these skills are considered valuable and attractive, and every other Bdsm person will want to be their friend.

Chapter Eleven

How To Tie Rope Without A Partner

This chapter will show you how to create a model if you do not have a partner. We will use a pool noodle and a sweatshirt and tie them on a chair to create some chest area.

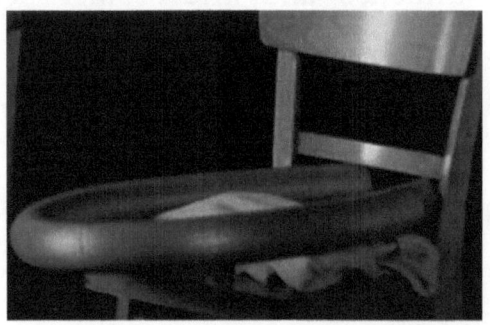

So you will be able to practice many things and some chest harnesses. It only simulates a square hand position on the chest, not anything complicated or fancy harnesses. However, it is a good start if you want to practice independently and do impossible things on your own. It is also an excellent way to practice the beginner course if you cannot do too many things on your legs. Some of the items will be on the legs. They may not be possible for everyone, especially if you are not flexible enough or if this is uncomfortable for you. Or simply if you do not have the desire to tie yourself up.

You may want to sit on a chair while doing this because when you practice on yourself. So, without a model, whether on this practice chair or yourself, this might be a more comfortable setup than sitting directly on the floor. So, even if you are tying things on your leg or even using two chairs, tying on your knee might be a lot more comfortable and accessible than sitting on the floor and having to bend over or kneel for a long time.

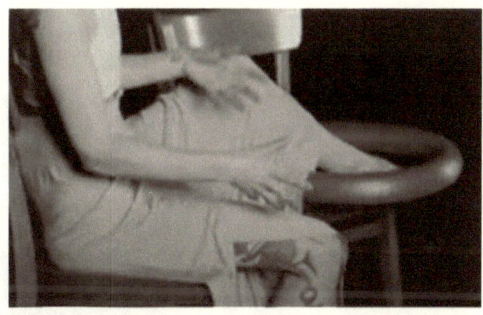

Hopefully, that will be helpful for you, and it will allow you to practice many things more comfortably and get ready to tie yourself or your partners.

How to create the practice chair

You are going to need this pool noodle, and this is something you can buy in a local store or online. It costs about three to four dollars, and this is just a standard one, so there is no need to buy something fancier.

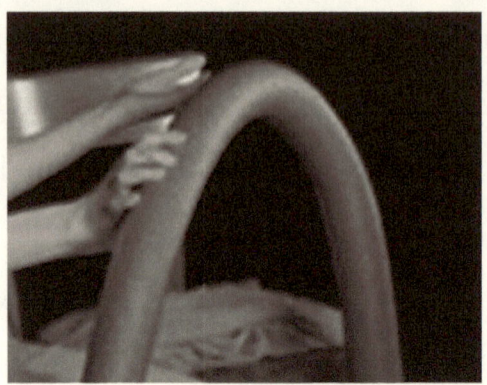

And then you are going to need a sweatshirt. It would help if you had a sweatshirt that is wide enough that it is going to cover as much of the pool noodle as possible.

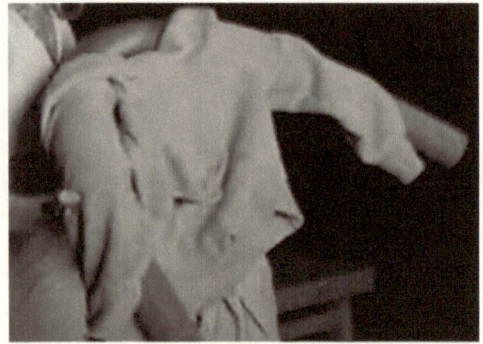

Pull the noodle through the arms of the sweatshirt on both sides and roughly to the middle.

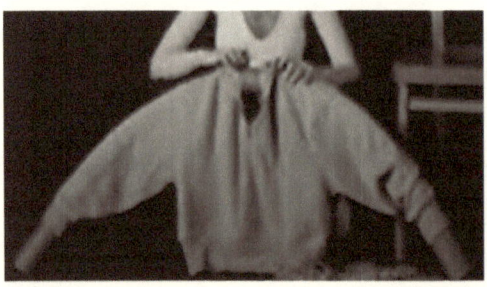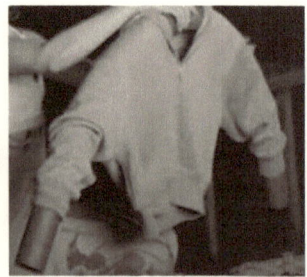

And then put the sweatshirt over the chair. But, again, according to the kind of chair you have, it might make more sense to have it in the front or the back.

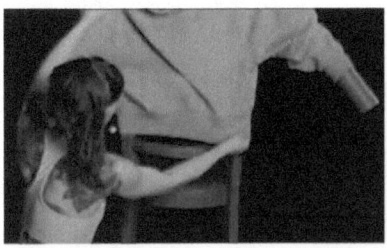 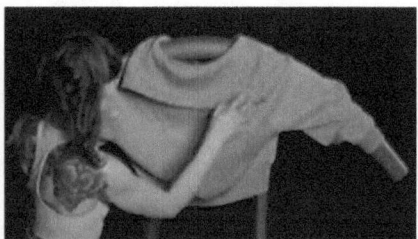

But have a way to keep the pool noodles on top and towards the front.

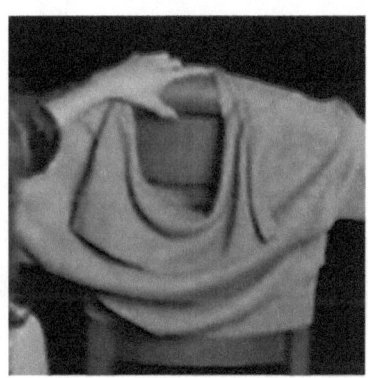

Ensure this is in the middle so the arms are the same length on both sides. It tends to fall and move around a lot, so the first thing you may want to do is take a little piece of rope; this does not have to be bondage. It can be anything you have around the house to lock in place.

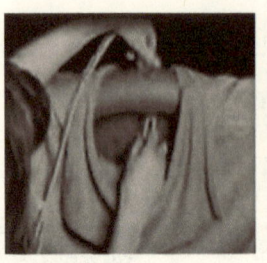 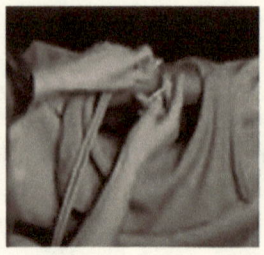 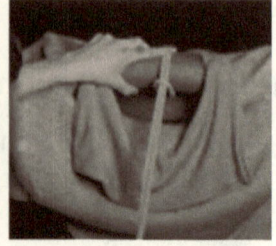

Try to get it a little more stable onto the top of the chair, so just wrap it around a few times quite tightly until you feel like it is solid.

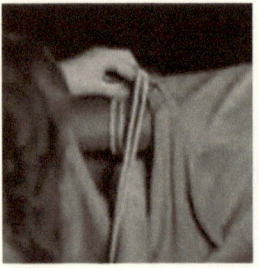 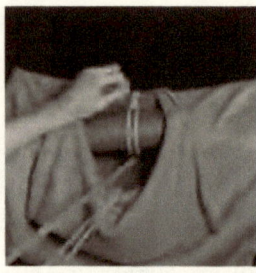 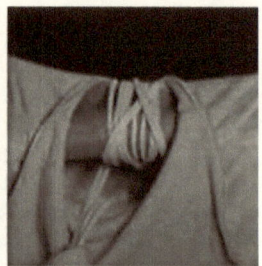

Once you feel it is enough, close it in the back

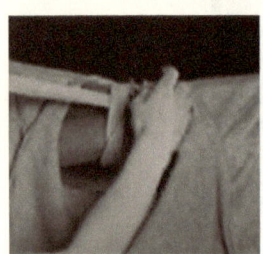 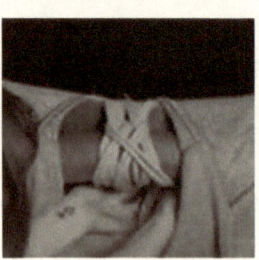 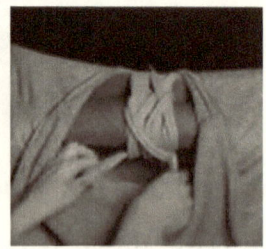

And just lock it in place. Once you are done, close the little zipper so it looks nice, and folds the neck part inwards.

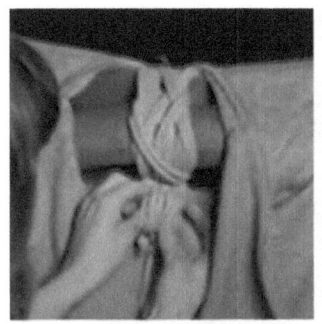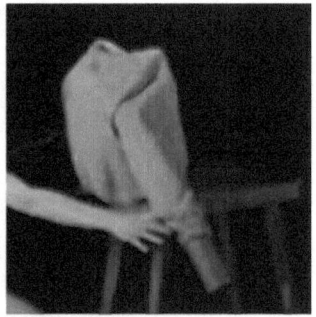

So, now you can start pulling the arms in to finish the position.

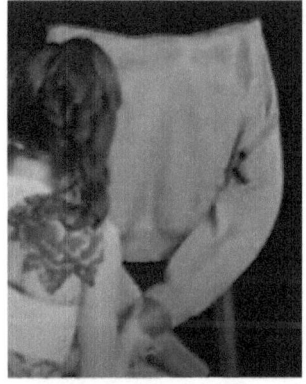

It may be hard if you try to keep the extensions of the pool noodle in place and tie something to it. It is always going to come off, and it is tricky.

So, an effortless way is to retake small pieces of rope. It does not have to be bondage rope, but it can be anything, and catch yourself onto the pool noodle.

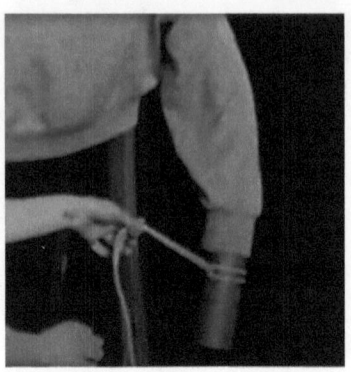

So, it is pretty good to be straight onto it and not on the fabric because this plastic creates friction, so it stays in place nicely.

Pull the lark's head tightly, bend the arm, and then go on the opposite side of the chair and tie it off; so just go around this part of the chair and the noodle a couple of times until you are running out of rope and you can just close this off.

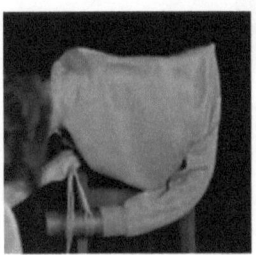
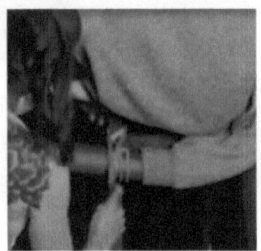
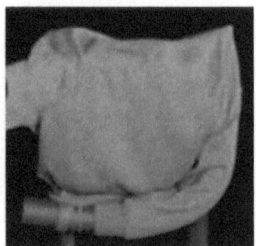

You can do this in any way; there is no safety issue here, so anything that works and drops the sweater on top covers the rope.

Do the same thing, on the other hand, the same principle. Do a lark's head again, put it onto the little arm, pull it tight, and bend it to the other side. Again, look for the chair part to stop the rope from sliding down. If you do it on the lower section, it will always slide down. So, make sure you come up, catch the arm with the rope, and pull the arm up. And again, just loop around from the chair to the noodle until you are running out of rope, and then you can close it and cover it up.

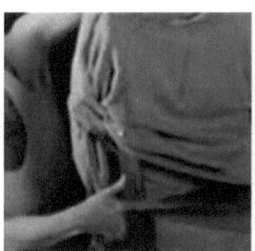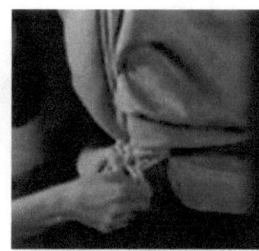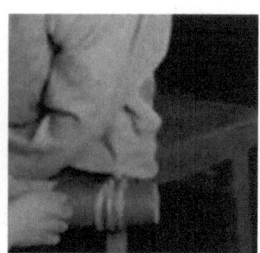

Ensure you can use the arms; you may have to push things a little higher and adjust the noodles.

Maybe you can make it slightly less tight and leave more space. According to your chair and setup, it will be slightly different, but you have a chest and can practice all sorts of things from there.

You can practice the single and double-column ties around the wrist or the TK, frictions, and all sorts of things on ties.

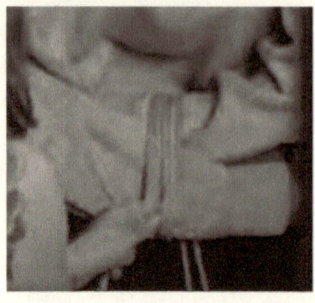 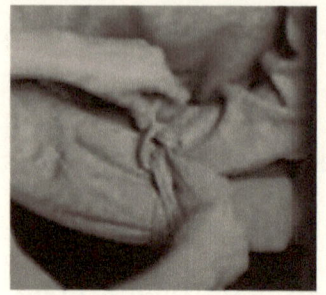

You can even do Hojo cups because you have isolated arms or wrap them all around it.

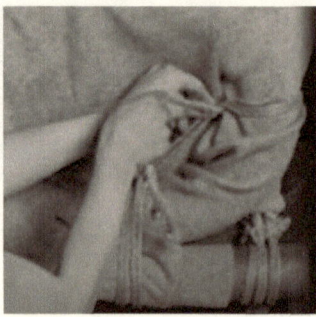 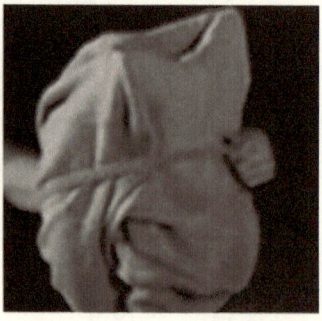

The nice part of it is that the noodle is going to create this kind of squishy feeling that a natural body is going to have. So, if you do the same thing without the noodle and throw a sweatshirt onto a chair, it will have sharp and hard surfaces like this, the rope will slide around, and it will not feel the same.

You also sense how it feels to put tension onto a body.

You can find this helpful trick. It will allow you to practice your frictions or some new harnesses quietly and relax even if you do not have a partner.

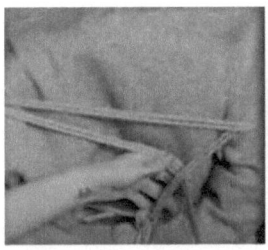 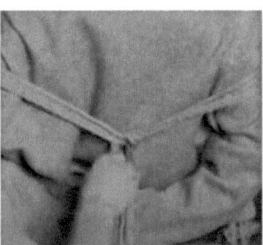 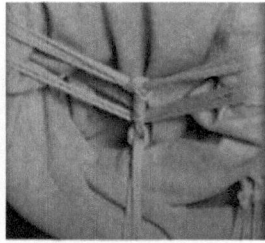

Chapter Twelve

Basics of Suspension Points

This chapter discusses how to install a suspension point. It is the hard point for the suspension; typically, you would want the actual hard point installed by a proper builder or engineer or come off a properly built frame. So that you know the fundamental structure of the thing you are coming off is appropriately installed. The techniques for doing this differ between wood and concrete ceilings; that part needs professional knowledge.

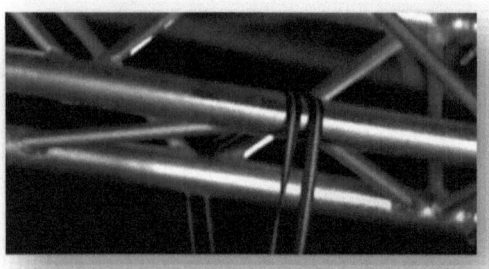

There are also cases where the ceiling in your house is a dropped ceiling, a suspended ceiling we call it, which is the case quite commonly when you have recessed lighting. So that ceiling is fake. It is just plasterboard, and the entire ceiling is just above that one. So, you do need to get that part done by a professional.

That point should be as high up as possible in a traditional house. So you are looking at a point being maybe two and a half meters off the ground. That Is too high to reach, and so what we do is we drop a hard point down from that. We drop using a sling so that a standard climbing sling can be doubled over several times or just using the rope. And to use the rope, you can build a standard suspension line; make sure it is firm because that line is crucial. It is the fundamental part of all of your suspensions after that.

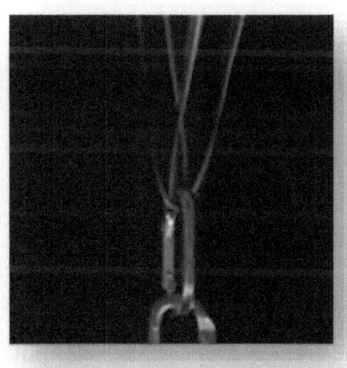

Some people prefer using a sling because they tend to stretch less than rope, which saves much effort. Plus, if you are doing photography work, you can usually have it high enough that you do not see what is suspending the point. In this example case, we have a sling with two carabiners below it.

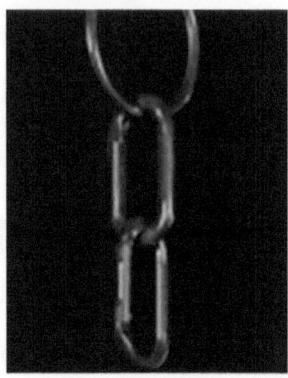

A hardpoint carabiner will place other carabiners or even a ring.

Comparing suspension points

You can use carabiners, a ring, or bamboo to set up your suspension point on your hardpoint.

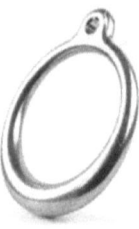 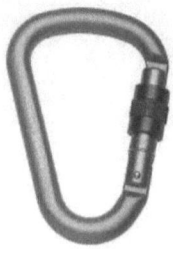 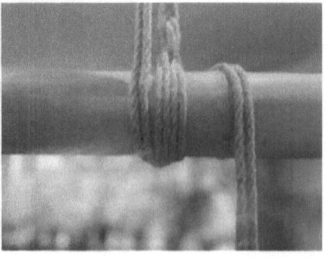

This relatively thin ring, attached with a swivel, is a good size of the ring; it gives you plenty of space to secure your points.

And those points will come together to form a conical suspension.

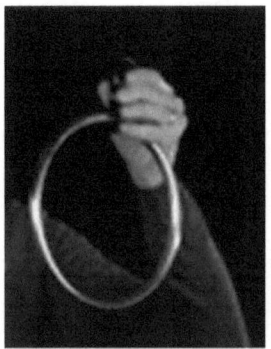

The height of the person from this ring also matters. The closer they are to the ring, the more compressed the suspension and the closer the tie. But, again, that matters a lot when dealing with ties that affect flexibility, for example, compressing the back.

Carabiners are similar to a ring. The technique is to use a separate carabiner for every one of your main lines, whereas on a ring, one ring typically has all the main lines. There will eventually be a problem with space on a ring, but this is also an advantage in the beginning because it stops you from using too many main lines simultaneously. Typically, on a ring, you want to use maybe three complete four suspension lines at any time.

Another advantage of carabiners is that they allow you to work at multiple heights. So, with carabiners, you can daisy chain them by connecting multiple carabiners to lower your suspension point just for a single line. Typically, you will not have more than one suspension line per carabiner. It is very important to make sure that you do not collide. Also, be careful when tightening your suspension line on the carabiner so the lines do not jump on each other. One way to do that is to ensure that the lines run in the same direction, not opposite. The same is true in a ring, but the effect is slightly less pronounced.

The diameter of the ring also matters. Some rings are thicker, while others are thin. A thin ring puts slightly more pressure on the rope because it has to go over a tighter curve. The thicker ring uses up more rope, so you will notice that your main lines seem a bit shorter than they were on a thick ring.

Wood versus metal also makes a big difference. A metal ring is heavy, but the lines move far more smoothly. If lines are smooth to go up, it is easy to increase the height of a tie to pull it up, but it is also faster to come down. So you have to ensure that you are careful when you are coming down when using a metal ring. A wooden ring is a gymnastic ring roughly the same size but has a broader diameter. Those rings have a lot more friction, and you will generally find locking off a lot easier, but you will also find that increasing the height of your tie requires a bit more effort. So there is a compromise there. Just be aware of the properties of each piece of material, and you will be fine,

A typical piece of bamboo can also serve for suspension. We would typically suspend this from both ends, requiring two independent suspension points. To be suspended, you would suspend it as close to the level as possible. The bamboo is thicker than the wooden ring and the carabiner setup. So, you would usually suspend this slightly lower because your lines will go over it more. That wider diameter uses up more rope. The lock-offs are also different on bamboo. For a typical diameter of bamboo, you would not want to go much thinner for suspension, and you can go thicker.

Bamboo also splits; it is a natural material and has imperfections. For example, you may see a split formed along the length of the bamboo.

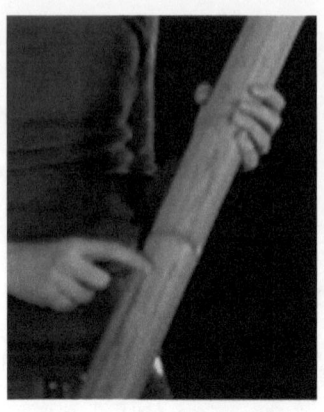

Do not worry much about weakening the bamboo, But it can damage the rope over it. So, if you suspend a piece of bamboo, check where the splits are. If they are all on one side, make sure that the side is facing downwards so that the top side of the bamboo where the lines are touching those parts is smooth and does not end up snagging or cutting the rope.

Setting up a sling

You may want to make your suspension point coming off an existing hardpoint like a trussing that has been structurally installed in this building. You might want to suspend it, but we would not come off it directly but would use a sling to make a suspension point below it. There are a couple of ways of doing that, but basically, it comes to going over and through something.

So, if you want to go over it, bring it to a central point where you can clip a carabiner, which is your suspension point.

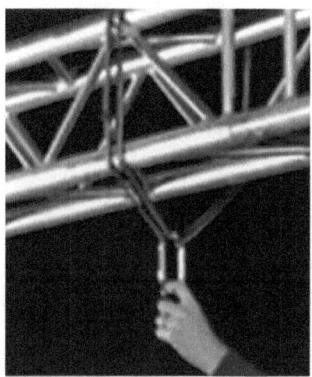

That is where you can use your hardpoint. You can build more carabiners off that point or add a ring. For example, you might use this carabiner setup to become your suspension line.

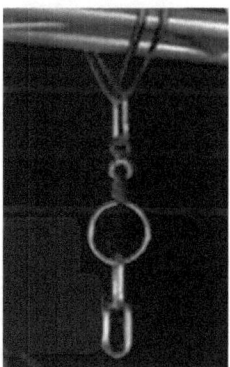

If you notice, as in this case, that your suspension line is a bit too high, maybe you want to make it longer, then you have a few choices. For instance, we can also go through trussing.

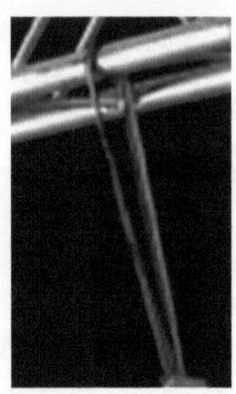

This does not need trussing; it could be a pre-installed ceiling ring like an eye loop. Then, take the sling and go through that, and you will notice that the point is lower because you are going around less. You can lock your head to the sling to lower it again.

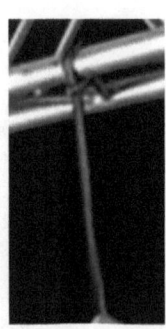

It is usually advised against because the swings are weaker in this configuration. But check with the manufacturer for Shibari, depending on the loads or the sling. But this is a way of having the sling be much lower down.

If you want to use the sling with a wooden or metal ring, you can use a carabiner setup to connect the ring and the strap.

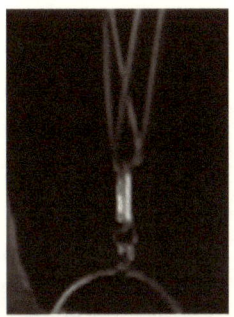

Suppose you did not have a pre-existing swivel or loop on the ring to do this with, for example, on a wooden ring. In that case, you can work by building a lark's head on the ring itself, going over your suspension point, and clipping these together with a carabiner.

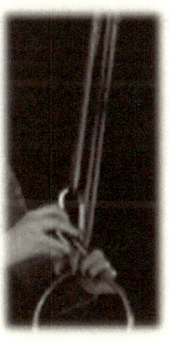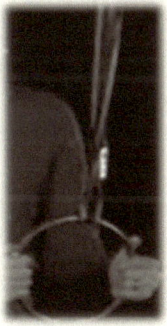

If you are using this method, you have clipped these two together. And a way of testing that if you are going to do something like this, you must pull down hard and pull yourself up to make sure it is working.

Another way to adjust the height is doing multiple wrap-around to use up some of the slings before clipping on your carabiner.

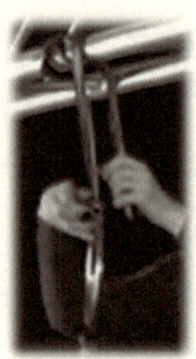

As a tip, especially with slings, never try to tie them off. You do not want to tie slings together as your lock-off; use a carabiner. The reason is that slings are designed to be used with carabiners and because the material they are made with is quite slippery. Therefore, they are not ideal for being tied.

Those are a few simple methods to suspend your ring or carabiner setup to a point.

Setting up a bamboo

In terms of actually suspending your bamboo, you need to do that at both points on the bamboo. And in terms of where you suspend from, that also matters. You may notice that you have these knuckles; if you suspended the bamboo to the side with no knuckles afterward, then there is a chance that your suspension point could fall off the end.

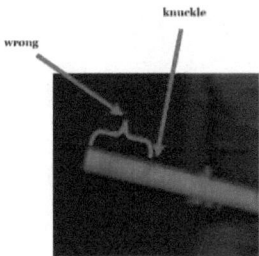

It is not ideal, so we tend to suspend it on the other side of a knuckle because it gives a bit of resistance to the bamboo coming down.

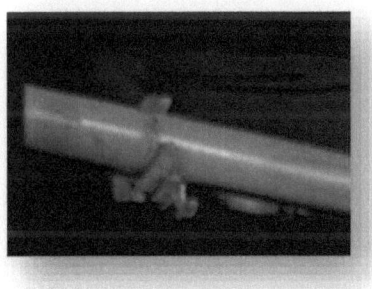

Sometimes, you might see people using a sling to suspend bamboo, but that is not good because it is not tight enough and tends to be slippery. So, suspend the bamboo using the rope.

There are multiple methods for doing this, but it involves tying a perfect single-column tie and then suspending that, maybe tying using a clove hitch.

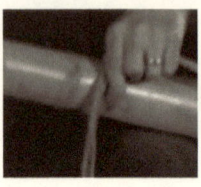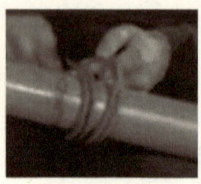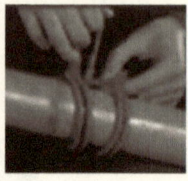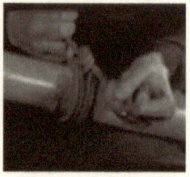

A clove hitch with a knot on top and then protecting the bight before suspending the bamboo is good. The clove hitch is very secure and gives much resistance to sliding.

We can go to the hardpoint and suspend it using standard lock-offs.

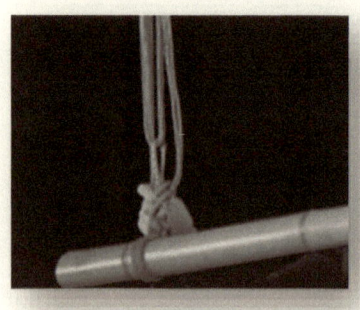

You can lock off the line with a mantra hitch and two half-hitches. Then, with an extra rope, you can use that on the bamboo before tying it off.

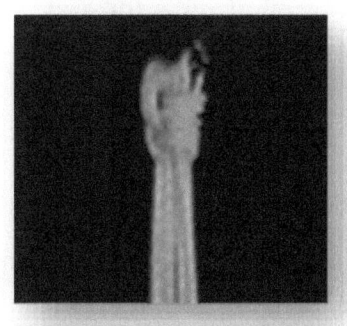 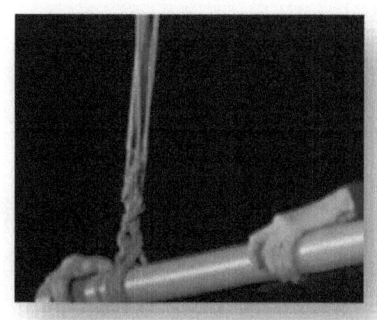

Using carabiners as your suspension hardware

There are different carabiners; some are better than others for suspension work.

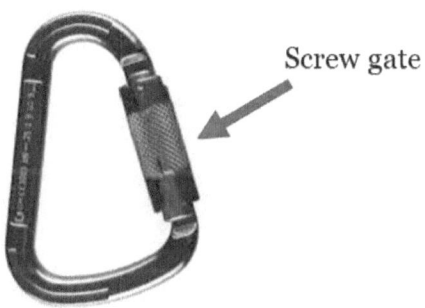

Screw gate

The image above shows an example of a carabiner that is good for setting up your hardpoint that fits well for everything above the suspension. But it is unsuitable for coming off. One problem is the screw gate. The screw gate is easy to jam, but it slows you down in a way that is not helpful. They are meant for climbing, for extra safety during a fall, but that sort of safety is not needed with the loads we are dealing with in Shibari. You will also notice that the bottom of it is very sharp in a v-shape. It means that your ropes will tend to bunch up together, and you stand more chance of having a jam or more chance of having ropes worn against each other and breakage. So, we do not recommend this type for your suspension mainline.

Instead, we suggest getting hold of a perfectly oval carabiner with the so-called straight gate.

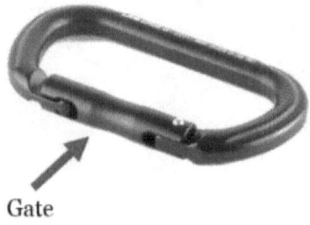

Gate

The oval ends mean you can come over either side, giving you plenty of space for your suspension lines without them getting together.

The gate on some does have a sharp piece, which is not ideal. But you must be careful not to run the rope through it. Those are perfect for suspension work if you can find carabiners with no hook and are blunt.

You have several choices regarding using a ring, and some rings have a swivel.

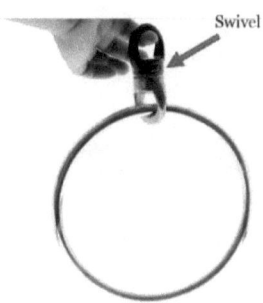

The swivel allows the ring to rotate freely. This advantage is that you can turn somebody smoothly for a very long time and stop them from spinning.

If you do not have a swivel, any twists in the sling, especially in a room with high ceilings, will travel down into your suspension. And you will end up with a person spinning indefinitely, making managing your suspension difficult. It is also challenging to do shots like a photo or a video shoot if you want them to face a particular way.

On the ring, you can clip carabiners, and the reason for this is to allow them to fan out more to give yourself more room so the carabiners can fan out like so and the cone effect is increased.

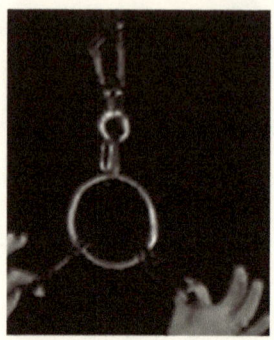

So, the apex of the cone is now higher up. You will also notice a carabiner slightly above the ring. You can all go through it with another carabiner. If you want to go higher, you can also place a carabiner.

The same technique can be used on a typical suspension ring where you place the carabiner through the gap in the swivel. But, again, it allows you to have slightly more height if you suspend where you might need that. So, this is a handy trick to keep in mind.

Demonstrating some carabiner management

Tie a single column tie around the ankle.

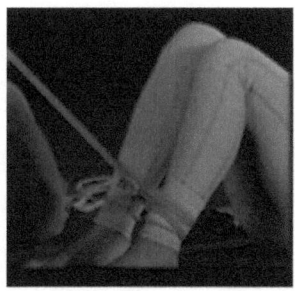

Next is going to the carabiner. Again, we recommend starting with two carabiners because it gives you more choices when adding more lines later.

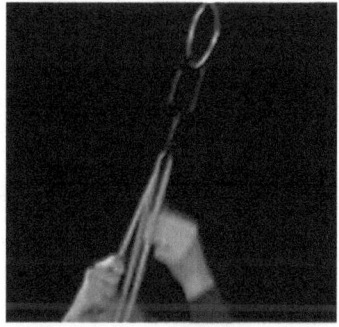

Remember when you go through to ensure that your lines are running in the same direction on the carabiner itself and locking off in a standard way. Using a mantra hitch followed by two half hitches and just something to tidy up the rope's end.

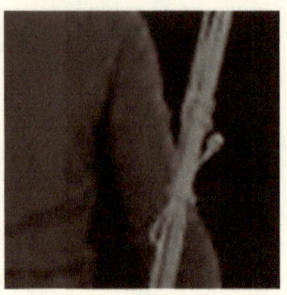

After you have gone through a carabiner, try not to put any more rope through that carabiner. So, if you want to add more lines, add them to the others. You may notice that a carabiner is very close to this knot. And you depend on the angle and height of the person, how close they are to the ring. That can create a jam and be very difficult for your fingers to get in. So we recommend making lock-offs about one carabiner's height below the previous carabiner.

It allows you to extend down while having clearance between carabiners and lock-offs. In this case, put the following line lower, building down the way.

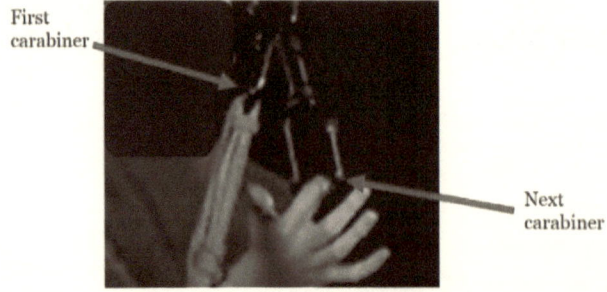

First carabiner

Next carabiner

And just using two-half hitches is sufficient if the line is not mainline.

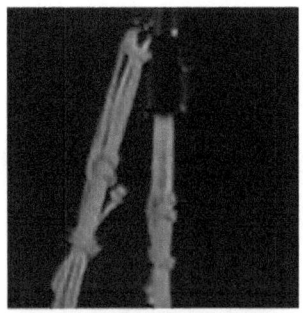

You can choose where to place it by continuing and adding one more line. However, the line appears too busy, so do not place a carabiner to cluster it. The best choice would be, unless you wanted more height, you might use the higher carabiner; for now, go to the ring.

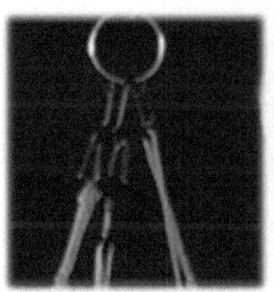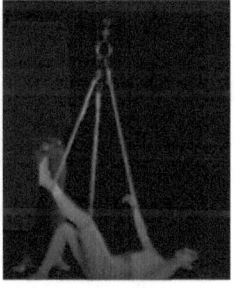

You may first notice that the lines are all pulled together on the carabiners. So the lines converge onto a single point, specific to single-point suspensions on a ring or carabiners. On bamboo, you can choose to do this if you want, but you can also have the lines spread apart; you have other choices. But on a carabiner setup, this is what you have.

It also means that the height of the person from the carabiners matters. If the model were higher, these lines would come in at a sharper angle, and there would be more of an effect compressing the body.

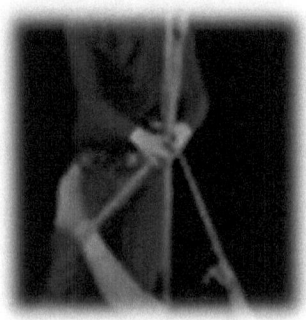

There is also more you can do with carabiners as a pulley.

You can also place a carabiner on the bottom, like a simple pulley, if you want smooth movement. You also have an advantage: putting it through the bight or the cuff. But also capture the bight for a bit of safety.

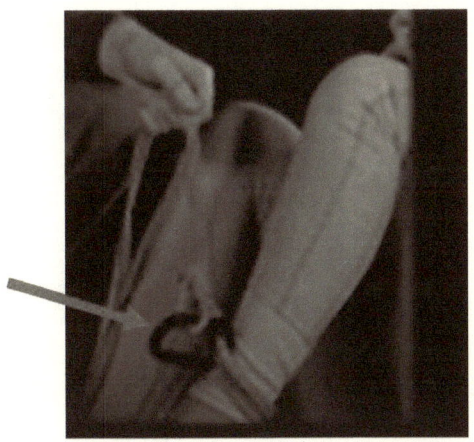

It gives you extra safety, and you can use this on a single-column tie and your wire hanger suspension. The movement is much smoother and faster to go up and down. It is another popular lock-off from carabiners because it is speedy to tie and also very fast to untie.

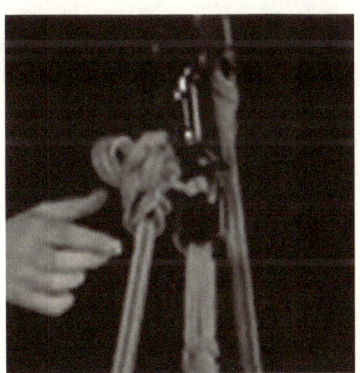

We do not suggest coming down by untying the knot because you are supporting all of the weight on a single rope and a single muscle group.

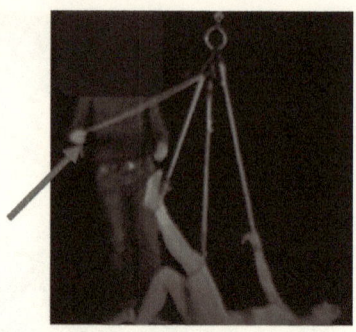

You are much better off using your hand as a break, particularly useful on heavier limbs.

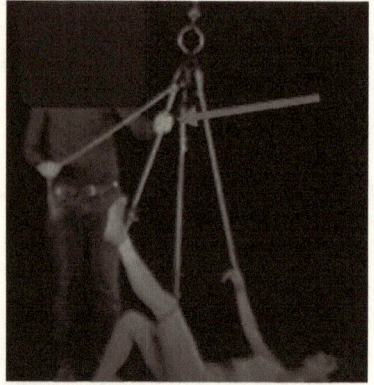

In this case, you will apply some weight, making that easier, but the control breaking comes from the hand squeezing the ropes together.

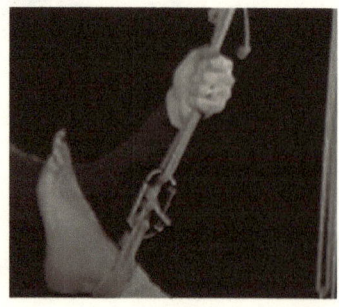

It is how the two half hitches work: squeezing the ropes together and generating much friction between the rope fibers.

Carabiners tend to make much noise if you leave them up. Therefore, we recommend that when working with carabiners, remove each carabiner as the line comes down from that carabiner.

In an emergency, you can take the carabiner down itself. However, you would have to have help to do this. But this can be useful if a line has jammed or if there is a reason why you cannot take the line down quickly.

Setting up a pulley

This method uses many carabiners and requires quite a lot of height. Therefore, it is not used very often, but it is helpful for some ties when you do not want to carry an actual pulley system around.

Pulleys place much stress on the rope used as a pulley; that rope is vital for the suspension. So make sure you are using a very new rope for this.

To start, take one of our carabiners and tie an overhand knot on the carabiner, leaving a small amount of rope as the bight.

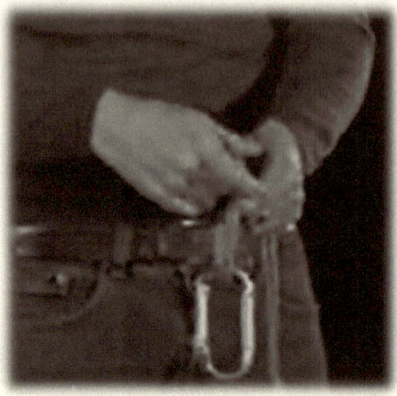

Place the bight through, so it is locked inside the carabiner.

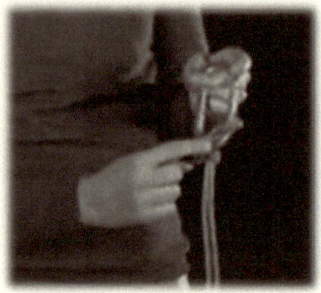

It means you will rely on the knot but have the lock as a backup. It also does not use too much space, which is necessary.

You want to use your carabiners in sets of two, so there is a carabiner at the bottom. Hold the first carabiner you placed and raise the other one to the point. It helps ensure that you do not have any twists in your lines, and you'll need to apply gentle pressure down the way to avoid this from spinning and tangling.

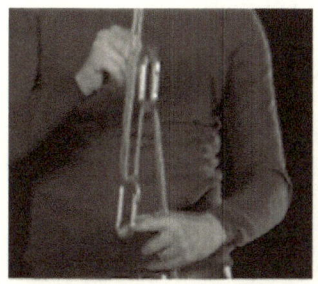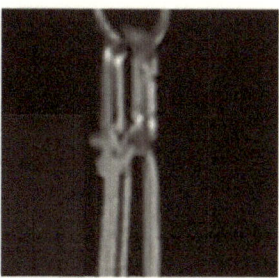

So, this forms a straightforward pulley system. But you can extend it again by taking another two carabiners, holding the middle one down, and raising the other to the ring.

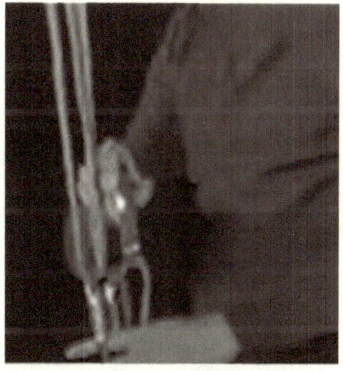

It gives you a two to three-pulley system; make sure the ropes are not rubbing against each other too much before using it.

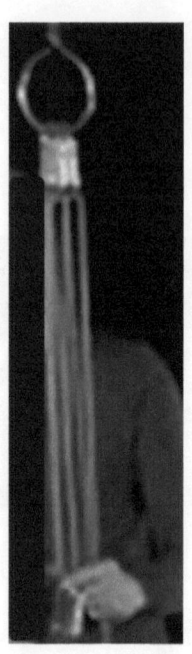

At the bottom is where you would place your actual carabiner.

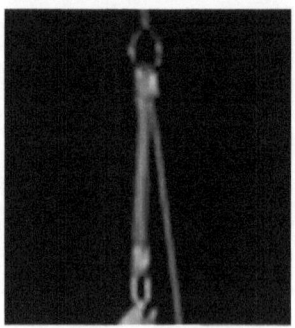

Lock it off the usual way, but be aware that moving is easy. There is not much friction, so you want to lock off properly.

Once the pulley is locked off, you can go through the carabiner and use your suspension line. Locking off in the usual way using two-half inches ensures your two pitches are very tight. Even then, you may want to come through and do something else at the bottom to ensure that things can not move.

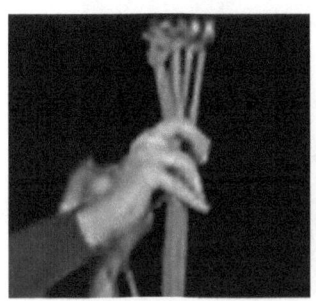 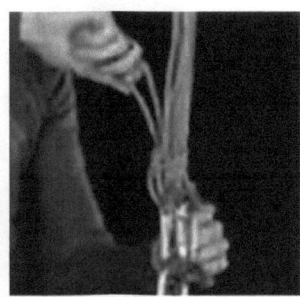

Once the hard point is solid, you can suspend the weight or model.

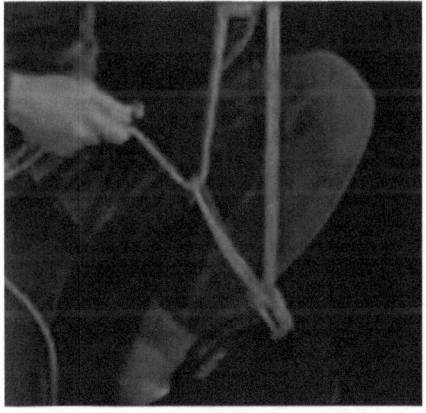

Unlike in a usual suspension where you would pull the weight off the ground, we can stop and suspend the weight using the pulley system to adjust the height of the suspension.

So it is much easier, you feel much less weight, and it is much easier to go up and down.

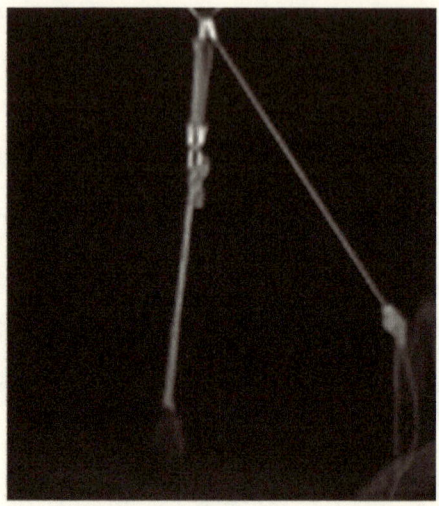

This technique is helpful for suspensions where you know the suspension will be very short-lived and want to come down to the ground quickly.

To come down, you would usually come to ground level, keeping a little tension on the line to make it easier to untie and undo your suspensions. It is recommended to focus on removing the lines from the person before taking your pulley system down. So, fully untie the person first, then you can deal with the ropes later.

Checking for Nerve Damage during a Bondage Scene

In this chapter, we will demystify what we mean by hand checks, when you need to be doing hand checks, and how to do the hand checks. So, first of all, we are trying to understand whether we have a nerve compression issue when talking about hand checks. We will have nerve compression issues, or most concerning, when a rope crosses the arms, wrists, or anywhere in between. So, if you are doing some suspension in a hands-free chest harness, you do not likely need to be worried about doing hand checks. On the other hand, suppose rope is not crossing your arms or not crossing your wrists. In that case, this isn't a time that you have to be concerned about nerve compression in the way we are worried about or how we're trying to decipher when we're doing hand checks.

One of the things we are trying to do when we check our hands is to understand the sensations we are feeling in our hands: circulation sensations or nerve sensations. And so, when our circulation becomes restricted, we feel the entire hand going to sleep. So there is a tingle, sometimes a feeling of lethargy or slowness. The feeling you might have if you fall asleep on your arm funding and you wake up with the

239

entire hand feeling numb or sitting in a class. Your leg has gone to sleep, and you must wake it back up; that is all over pins and needles.

Nerve impingement or nerve compression of compression feels quite different than that. So, nerve compression feels like a sensation isolated from your hand. And it is one of the things that we are trying to understand and feel for when we do our hand checks. Do my hands feel different on one side of the hand or the other?

So, there are two primary nerves we are concerned about when doing bondage. First, your radial nerve will innervate the outside of your thumb and the top of your hand a little bit; it innervates sensation. And then, depending on where it is crossing your body, it also innervates your ability to lift your wrist.

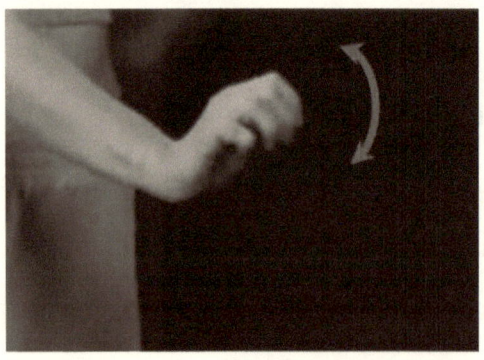

And you have your ulnar nerve; your ulnar nerve innervates sensation in the little finger.

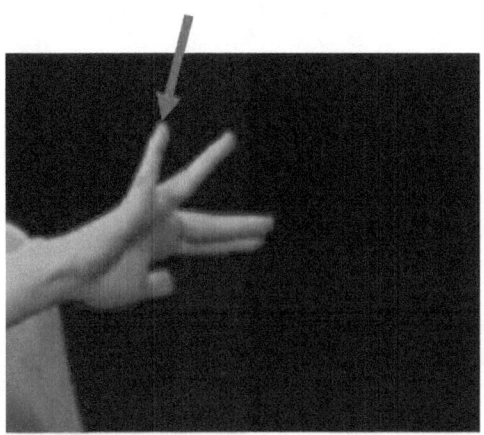

The ulnar nerve is responsible for some grip strength. So, the first thing we feel when we do hand checks is that we are testing whether the pinkie feels different from the rest of the hand and whether the thumb feels different from the rest. Not only does my hand feel tingly or my thumb or pinky feel tingly, but does it feel distinct? For instance, does it feel different if you rub the thumb than the other fingers? In some cases, you should also be able to test yourself for specific motor capacities. So, if you have your hands behind your back, you can push your hands into my back to test your ability to flex the wrist.

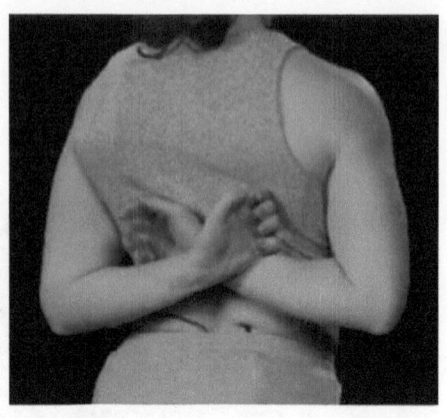

And even if your hand is a little bit circulation blocked, or it is hard for you to feel it in your hand, you can usually tune into the sensation in your back of pressure. You can feel it if you can flex firmly into your back with your hand. Suppose you have a rigger doing a hand check for you or asked your rigger to do a hand check for you. In that case, your rigger should be testing both directions of motor function, grip strength, and the ability to flex the wrist. It is never the riggers' job to test for sensation; that is your responsibility. Suppose your rigger puts a finger in your hand and asks you to squeeze. In that case, you also want your rigger to grab your hand so they can check your ability to open up against them, lift your thumb, and extend your hand.

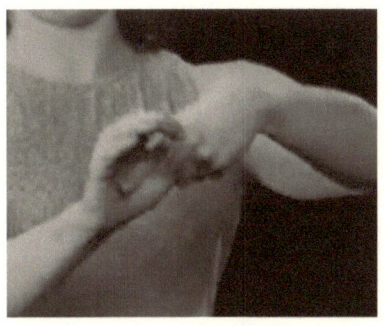 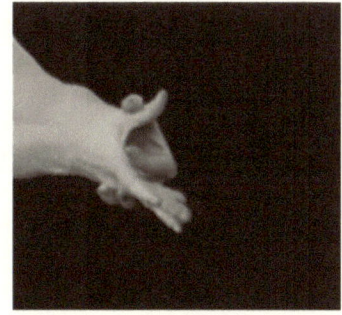

And that is the sort of thing your rigger should then be able to communicate to you whether your grip strength or ability to flex feels weak. Again, your grip strength usually indicates an ulnar problem, and the ability to bend typically indicates a radial nerve problem.

Conclusion

We have finally come to the end of this book. This book is a helpful motivation for getting into Shibari and would also guide you through the safety instructions you must follow. Shibari is a fantastic art; you will be a professional once you have learned about it. Now that you know how to do the Shibari art, why do not you try it? Finally, ensure you have learned all the safety precautions you must take. Have a wonderful experience!